Buying a Bike

Buying a Bike

How to get the best bike for your money

Rob van der Plas

CYCLING RESOURCES
books are published by
Van der Plas Publications, San Francisco

Printed in the U.S.A.

Published by:
Van der Plas Publications
1282 7th Ave.
San Francisco, CA 94122
U.S.A.

U.S. book trade sales:
Dan Haldeman & Associates
Watsonville, CA

Cover design:
Kent Lytle, Alameda, CA, using a photograph by Bob Allen

Photography:
Frontispiece photo by Bob Allen, Bozeman, MT;
all other photos by Neil van der Plas, San Francisco, CA

Publisher's Cataloging in Publication Data
Van der Plas, Robert, 1938 –
Buying a Bike: How to get the best bike for your money.
p. cm.
Includes bibliographical references and index.
1 Bicycles and bicycling—handbooks and manuals. I. Authorship.
II. Title.
L.C. Card No. 98-61190
ISBN 1-892495-17-1 (paperback original)

Acknowledgments

The author wishes to express his gratitude to A Bicycle Odyssey and Sausalito Cyclery (both in Sausalito, California) and American Cyclery in San Francisco, for making available several of the bicycles and components shown in the photographs.

Warning and Disclaimer

Cycling is associated with a certain level of risk. Although it is the author's intent to show the reader how to choose and handle the bike safely, no claim is made that this is a comprehensive manual for bicycle safety. In general, no amount of advice in itself can be as effective as thoughtful operation of the bike by the rider.

Although the author recommends wearing a helmet when cycling, no protective gear can protect the rider against all risks, and it should in general be seen as the rider's responsibility to use caution.

In case of uncertainty about the mechanical operation of the bike, and in case this book does not provide an adequate answer, consulting a bike shop is recommended, preferably the one where the bike was purchased.

Table of Contents

1. Introduction **9**

Where to Buy 10   Bicycle Brand Names 12
Types of Bikes 11   Other Criteria 13

2. Choosing a Bike Type **15**

Mountain Bikes 16   Hybrids 21
Road Bikes 19   Other Bikes 22

3. Understanding the Bicycle **29**

The Parts of the Bike 29   Know Your Gruppos 35

4. Sizing Your Bike **38**

Frame Size 39   Handlebar Height 41
What's Your Frame Size? . . 40   Front Length 42
Saddle Height 41   Other Dimensions 43

5. Other Equipment for You and Your Bike **45**

Gear for the Rider 45   Attachment and Removal
Gear for the Bike 48   of Accessories 52
                                 Tools and Spares 53

6. Buying a Used Bike **54**

Where to Buy a   Bike Theft and the
     Used Bike 55   Secondhand Market . . 55
                                 Checking It Out 56

7. Setting Up Your Bike **58**

Adjusting the Saddle 58   Remove and Install
Handlebar Adjustment . . . 61   Wheel 63
Brake and Gear Lever   Remove and Install
     Adjustments 63   Pedals 65

8. Using the Gears **67**

The Parts of the
    Derailleur System . . . 68
Gearing Theory 69
Gearing Practice 70

9. Getting Familiar with Your Bike **72**

Check It Out 73
Riding Practice. 73
Braking Practice 74
Steering Practice. 75
Different Terrain. 76

10. Safe Cycling **77**

Single Participant
    Accidents 78
Multiple Participant
    Accidents 79

11. Routine Maintenance **81**

Cleaning the Bike 82
Pre-Ride Inspection 82
Monthly Inspection 84
Seasonal Inspection 85

12. Basic Repairs **88**

Fixing a Flat 88
Patching a Tube 91
Fix Gear Shift Problems. . . 92
Tighten Loose Crank 93
Adjust Brake 94

Bibliography 95
Index 96

1

Introduction

SO YOU have decided to buy a new bike. Whether you're new to the sport or an old hand looking for a new steed, this book will help you go about it as effectively as possible. You'll get straightforward answers to the questions you might ask, and you'll learn what questions to ask in the bike shops you visit.

One thing you won't find here is a listing of all the makes and models of bikes available in different bike shops and other outlets where bikes are sold. However useful such a list may seem, it's very transitory information: much of the information will be outdated by the time the list is published. Models are dropped, specifications are changed, prices are revised, and availability may be uncertain. Besides, what you really want to know is which bike is best for you, rather than a general listing of all the bikes available.

Fig. 1.1. An assortment of new bikes (an Electra cruiser, a Bianchi hybrid, a Bianchi road bike, and a Breezer full-suspension mountain bike) waiting for buyers at a bike shop in California.

In this book, you'll learn what features to look for to get a bike that is most suitable for your kind of use. (Yes, it says "a bike," not "the bike," because there will be several makes and models that are suitable, and their pricing will be so competitive that only you will be able to make the right choice between them.

Where to Buy

Bikes, even quite sophisticated ones, are available at many different outlets. Bike shops, general sporting goods stores, mailorder catalogues, and department stores all offer bikes. My general advice is to deal only with full-service bike shops. All the other types of outlets have two problems: you don't get personal, informed service, and you probably can't go back to have things corrected or fixed (an exception being some of the better sporting goods stores that may have an in-house bike repair department, making them essentially full-service bike shops).

I don't recommend buying a complete bike from a mail-order catalogue, because size and fit are so critical on a bike that what seems right on paper may turn out to be wrong when you try it out. I've occasionally bought certain accessories that were not available from my regular bike shop from a mail-order firm, and it's astonishing how often even such simple things turn out not to match, or to be defective or disappointing. Although most mail-order houses take exchanges, it's often more hassle than it would be to just go down to a bike shop and get it there—even if the price may be a little higher.

Not all bike shops are the same. Different stores may carry different brands; they may specialize in a particular type of bike; they may address a different type of clientele; or they may simply have a different attitude or philosophy.

If you are buying a new bike, you want a shop where they'll take you seriously and try to find what's best for *you*, rather than make a quick sale. If you're an advanced rider, you want a shop where the staff will accept your input and work with you to come up with something that matches your taste and experience.

Good bike shops treat their customers with respect, take time to answer questions, and enjoy repeat business from loyal customers. Jacquie Phelan, the famed pioneer of women's mountain biking, gives some tongue-in-cheek advice for finding a good bike shop in her contribution to my book, *The Original Mountain Bike Book.* Here it is in condensed form:

"Take a yardstick and stand against a door jamb, mark off your height and measure it. Remember this number in inches or centimeters. Then, with no intention of buying a bike, walk into the store, peruse the bikes, and hang out at the counter. You're simply testing the particular shop for its warmth—a great indicator of its ability to serve you. When someone asks if they can help you, say the usual, 'No, I'm just looking, thanks.'

"Now leave the shop, run back to your doorway, and measure your new height, after interacting with the shop. If the number is smaller than what you originally measured, find a new shop—those people rely on the brilliant tactic of humiliation to demonstrate their awesome bike knowledge. If the number is equal to or greater than your original height, it's a good shop. Head back there and buy a bike. They are happy to share their enthusiasm, even if you are just a fledgling and don't know what it's all about. I don't believe that the brand of bike is as important as the attention given to fit and follow-up. Excellent service is what you really need from a shop."

The message is simple: a bike shop where you feel respected is likely to give you the attention and personal service you deserve. Find such a shop, but don't be shy about shopping around, and if one shop has a nice attitude, but not the right bike for you, find another shop—one that has both the attitude and the bike you want.

Types of Bikes

Walk into a bike shop and the odds are that what you see are mountain bikes, mountain bikes, and more mountain bikes. But that does not mean there aren't plenty of choices available, and you certainly don't have to settle for a generic bike that's indistinguishable from everybody else's. In fact, there probably are more different types and subtypes of bikes available these days as at any time in the past. (Only 20 years ago, you could have walked into that same shop and found ten-speeds, ten-speeds, and ten-speeds, and much less variety than there is today.)

Not only are there other models available, the mountain bike itself comes in more variants than meets the eye at first. In Chapter 2, I will show you what's out there and how you can decide what is most suitable for your purpose. This will all be treated in the most general terms, while in the chapters that follow, we'll first learn to speak the language of cycling and then take a close look at the various parts that make up the bicycle, and how they differ for various types of bike.

The idea is of course not to get just any bike, but one that suits you. There is no such thing as a universal "best buy" for everybody. What is good for you may not be for the next person, nor indeed for you five years from now, when your interest in cycling has evolved. Think about the way you're going to use the bike—on the road, off-road, or both; daily, weekly, or infrequently; long distances or short trips; commuting, touring, training, or racing. Explain that to the sales personnel in the shops you visit, so they know what direction to steer you.

Bicycle Brand Names

There are literally dozens of different bicycle makes out there, both big and small. Actually, in terms of numbers of bikes produced, the respectable manufacturers whose wares are sold through the bike trade are small compared to some of the manufacturers represented elsewhere. The largest bike trade brands are Trek, Cannondale, and Specialized, while Trek

Fig. 1.2. Similar bikes, different makers. These midrange cross-country type mountain bikes from Breeze Cycles, Voodoo, and Marin have many things in common.

actually owns several other, smaller brand names, such as Gary Fisher, Klein, and LeMond.

Whether you buy a bike of one brand or another does not matter very much. In a given price category, they all offer similar quality, and they have all installed components from the same limited number of suppliers. They may differ a little in frame geometry (the sizes and angles of the various tubes of the bike's frame), in cosmetics, and sometimes in materials (today, many major manufacturers make only aluminum frames, some use only steel, while others have different model ranges using different materials).

Other Criteria

At least as important as the type of bicycle are its quality and size, but also highly personal criteria can matter. The various types of bikes are described in Chapter 2. The issue of correctly sizing a bike will be addressed in some detail in Chapter 4. The other criteria will be discussed here.

Personal preferences are perfectly legitimate. If you don't like the color, a particular manufacturer's name, or the model designation on an otherwise perfectly suitable machine, then you may never get used to it. You'll get more fun out of cycling if you avoid that particular bike. Ask at the bike shop—or at several different shops—what other makes, models, and colors are available in that particular category, and select one you like.

Fig. 1.3. Get a bike that fits you. These two Bianchi road bikes are representative of the wide range of sizes available for high-end bikes.

Weight is another factor. By and large, a lighter bike is nicer to ride, all else being the same. But sometimes weight may be saved at the expense of other more important criteria. The major one of these "other criteria" is usually cost: shedding pounds on a bike is a very expensive business. See whether you can live with a bike that's just a pound heavier and save yourself a bundle, or invest some of the money you save on a slightly heavier machine in an upgrade, such as extra accessories you want, a more comfortable helmet, or something else that's important to you.

Quality is of course the most important criterion, but how can you judge it? The first rule of thumb is that, within limits, you get what you pay for. If two bikes look similar but one is 50 percent more expensive than the other, it's unlikely that the cheaper one is just a better deal: more likely, the more expensive machine is simply the better product. The frame on the more expensive bike may be lighter or more accurate, the components may be of a higher quality material, or they may be more accurately machined. Ask what the differences are and how important they are for your particular kind of use.

2

Choosing a Bike Type

EVEN THOUGH mountain bikes are so prevalent as to dominate most bike shops these days, there is still plenty of choice. I've divided the total crop of available bicycles into a manageable number of different categories, with some sub-categories. They are listed here in approximate order of prevalence. You may never have seen some of the last models listed before, but they're all deserving of some attention.

1. Mountain bikes
   a. cross-country bikes
   b. downhill bikes
   c. recreational bikes

2. Road bikes
   a. conventional road bikes
   b. time-trialing and triathlon bikes

3. Hybrids
   a. regular hybrids
   b. trekking bikes
   c. city bikes

4. Touring bikes

5. Cruisers

6. Utility bikes

7. Roadsters and three-speeds

8. Cyclo-cross bikes

9. Fixed gear bikes
    a. track racing bikes
    b. fixed gear road bikes

10. BMX and trials bikes

11. Folding bikes

12. Tandems

13. Recumbents and hand cycles

In the following sections, we'll take a close look at each of these different types of bicycle, with the objective of finding the right model for you.

Mountain Bikes

This is clearly the most common type of bicycle these days. It's the bike to choose if you plan to ride on unpaved trails a lot. Fat knobby tires, flat handlebars, and wide-range multi-speed gearing are the major characteristics of any mountain bike. There is a wide variety of these machines, ranging from models designed for the masses to those intended for the truly devoted. They range in price from a few hundred dollars (the cheapest acceptable quality mountain bikes sell for about $300 in U.S. currency, $400 in Canada, £200 in Britain) to bikes costing literally ten times as much. They come in a range from those intended for casual use to those suitable for aggressive

Fig. 2.1. Cross-country mountain bike. This Pine Mountain model from Marin has a front suspension fork only.

competition, from models without any form of suspension to those with complex suspension systems front and rear.

It has become common to distinguish between two categories of "real" mountain bike: cross-country and downhill. The simpler fat-tire bikes for less ambitious riding are referred to as recreational bikes. The latter typically have a wider seat, a higher handlebar position, and smoother tires that are more suitable for riding on pavement than on dirt. These days, even many recreational bikes are equipped with front suspension.

Cross-country bikes are not just to ride across open terrain, but are suitable for virtually any kind of use. Downhill bikes are not much fun unless you're doing what they're best at—riding downhill fast. Cross-country bikes may or may not have front suspension, and if they have a rear suspension at all, it will have modest travel (the distance by which it can go up or down). Downhill bikes invariably have suspension front and rear, as well as extra powerful brakes, such as disk brakes (which almost invariably cause drag while riding, making them unsuitable for anything but descending). Cross-country bikes typically have a wider range of gearing than downhill bikes, making them more suitable for steep hill-climbing.

Front suspension alone can add anything from $50 to $400 to the cost of a bike, depending on the level of sophistication of the front forks. Bikes without rear suspension are referred to as "hardtails." Rear suspension adds another $100 to $500 to the cost of a non-suspension bike of the same quality. So, clearly, if you don't really need the suspension, you can save yourself a significant amount by doing without.

Fig. 2.2. Typical full-suspension mountain bike. This Ganzo model from Voodoo is a cross-country bike suitable for moderate downhill competition.

Front suspension has now become so common that within a short time, it may become hard to find a mountain bike without it. There are certainly uses for bikes with and without. Unless you ride on very rough surfaces a lot—be they unpaved trails or cobblestone roads—you don't need suspension. Suspension components need a lot more maintenance than any other parts of a bike, and they also can be a real headache if they are worn or damaged. They differ a lot in their maintenance needs, with some requiring maintenance after as little as 20 hours of riding. Ask at the bike shop to see the maintenance requirements of the model you're thinking of—and look elsewhere if it needs to be maintained too frequently.

On bikes without suspension, the tire pressure does the same job. By inflating the tires more or less, you can control not only how comfortable the bike is on the terrain you're dealing with, but also the amount of traction when accelerating, climbing, cornering, or braking. The thicker the tire, the more flexibility you have in those adjustments.For general use on unpaved trails, a tire diameter of 2.125 inches is considered optimal for general use on unpaved trails, while narrower tires may be fine if you ride mainly on paved roads and paths. Keep in mind that your choice should not necessarily be determined by the average but by the extremes—choose a bike that's equipped for the worst terrain you'll be riding.

Mountain bike brakes are controlled from easily accessible levers, and those brakes are powerful. In fact, they're often so powerful that they can be dangerous to the novice used to the ineffective brakes on the bikes he remembers from the past.

Fig. 2.3. Typical recreational bike. Like most other bikes in its class, this Bobcat Trail model from Marin has no suspension. Bikes like this are designed for an upright riding position.

Apply the front brake suddenly with full force, and chances are the rear wheel lifts off. (The thing to do in response is to back off on the lever for the front brake.) In Chapter 9, "Getting Familiar with Your Bike," I'll show you how to achieve the control needed to ride safely.

Road Bikes

A road bike is what used to be referred to as a "ten-speed" until the mountain bike became the dominant variety of bicycle in America. It's the bike to use if you ride mainly for fitness, sport or recreation on roads rather than on unpaved trails. The two main categories of road bike are conventional road bikes and special time-trialing and triathlon machines.

Special triathlon and time-trialing machines are built only for speed and not for maneuverability. The conventional road bike is the safer one to choose if you will be riding in traffic and among other cyclists a lot. You don't lean forward as much as on the triathlon bike, resulting in a slight aerodynamic disadvantage, but you'll have a lot better control over the bike and a better view of the road ahead. Except for the most expensive special triathlon and time-trialing bikes, most bikes sold for that purpose are regular road bikes to which triathlon bars have been added, and these are more versatile than the specialty bikes that some of the champions choose for triathlon and time trials.

Fig. 2.4 Modern road bike. This Titanium 4X model from Eddy Merckx has an American-made titanium frame built by Litespeed and is equipped with Shimano's Ultegra components.

The road bike has skinny tires, usually of the size 700 C, and I shall save you the explanation why they're not 700 mm (28 inches) in diameter, but only about 675 mm (27 inches). Their thickness can be anything from 18 mm (less than ¾ inch) to 32 mm (1¼ inches). All those tires will fit on the same rim size. (Real racing bikes may use special so-called sew-up or tubular tires, which are mounted on special rims.) Although the narrowest tires generally are the lightest, and offer the least rolling resistance, you should select thicker tires if you plan to ride on surfaces that are less than perfectly smooth. The narrowest tires must also be kept inflated very hard to minimize the risk of damaging them—making them even harder on rough roads. If high speeds are your thing—whether for triathlon, time-trialing, road racing or just for the hell of it—you'll want the skinniest and lightest tires, inflated to a high pressure.

For smaller riders, there are other tire sizes, but the frame has to be built around the particular tire size, and that puts them into the category of custom-built bikes. The available alternate sizes are 650 C (about 26 inches diameter) and 600 C (about 24 inches diameter). In addition to custom frames, there are only a few manufacturers who offer quality road bikes in those sizes suitable for small women and youngsters.

The other main characteristic of a road bike is the use of drop handlebars. They may seem uncomfortable at first, but they actually are more comfortable than flat bars in the long run. This is the reason why long-distance tourists and others who ride continuously for two hours or more tend to prefer them over straight handlebars. Their comfort is mainly due to the fact that you can hold them in many different ways—on top near the middle, in the bends above the brake levers, on top of the brake levers, or low at the ends. You can change the hand position, and as they say, "a change is as good as a rest." Triathlon bikes will have either special handlebars or regular drop bars with a forward extension that allows you to lean forward very far and keep your body very low. This increases the risk of a pitchover accident, so don't apply the front brake suddenly in this position.

The brakes on a road bike are harder to reach and operate than they are on a mountain bike, but once you've got the knack of it, you'll find them quite adequate.

The gears—usually 16 or 18, rather than the ten that came on the original ten-speed—can be operated either from shifters integrated with the brake levers on the handlebars, or from separate shifters mounted on the side of the frame's down tube. The pedals on most road bikes are of the clipless variety, meaning they must be used with dedicated cycling shoes that have matching clip-on cleats in the soles.

Hybrids

About five years into the mountain bike craze, some manufacturers took note of the fact that most of their customers didn't really ride their mountain bikes off-road a lot. That's how they came up with the idea of creating the hybrid. It's a bike that combines some of the mountain bike's characteristics in a package that is easier to ride on the road. If that's the use you'll give your bike, today's hybrid bikes bear looking into.

Most manufacturers of mountain bikes also offer hybrids in the same price range as their cheaper mountain bike models—usually about $300 to $600 depending on the quality of the components installed. They'll look similar to a mountain bike but with somewhat narrower and less knobby tires, and a more upright rider position. Most hybrids are equipped to allow mounting racks, fenders, and other gadgets that make a bike more practical for utilitarian use. Hybrid bikes usually have 700 C tires, but with a much thicker diameter and a lot more rubber than those used for road bikes.

The concept was refined in Europe, and some of those bikes evolved into what are called trekking and city bikes. Trekking

Fig. 2.5. Typical hybrid bike. Like other hybrids, this Boardwalk model from Bianchi is most suitable for recreational and transportational riding on roads or paved paths and smooth trails.

bikes are hybrids designed for touring use. They have sturdy luggage racks, and often fenders, lights, and an integrated lock. City bikes are similar and are intended for urban commuting, shopping and everyday transportation.

Like the mountain bike, the hybrid has wide-range gearing, flat handlebars, and powerful brakes. The same warning mentioned for mountain bikes applies here too: get used to the way those brakes operate so you develop a feel for their behavior.

Other Bikes

Although mountain bikes, road bikes, and hybrids together account for the lion's share of all bicycles sold these days, there are quite a few other models. These will be described briefly in the sections that follow.

Touring Bikes

A touring bike is similar in appearance to the road bike, but with the wide range gearing, powerful brakes, and sturdy tires of the hybrid. In addition, it is equipped with braze-ons for racks. Few manufacturers have been offering them recently, but they seem to be making a bit of a comeback. A good touring bike is of course also suitable for other kinds of riding. They are designed and built to be stable and comfortable on long distances, and to carry luggage safely. They vary in price from about $600 for an adequate mass-produced touring bike, to $2,500 for a high-end version.

If you really want to go touring a long way from home, the bike should not be too sophisticated. When you're a hundred miles from the nearest bike shop, or that shop is in a primitive country where bikes are not fancy toys but simple amenities, you won't be able to get replacement parts for anything but the simplest components. So in that case, forget about clipless pedals, integrated brake-and-gear levers, high-power battery lighting, even cartridge bearings. Get the simplest, most straightforward equipment available. Just make sure it's durable, and above all, serviceable.

Cruisers

Cruisers are back, or so it seems. These bikes with fat tires, a broad saddle, and wide handlebars are intended for laid-back, unambitious riding over short distances. They're not very comfortable, and they are not very suitable for climbing hills, riding fast, or riding far. They appeal to the nostalgic sentiments of America's kids in their late forties and fifties. It's an OK bike to get if you just want to ride short distances and like the feeling that comes with this kind of bike.

Although department store cruisers today are no better than the originals, many bike shops sell cruisers that are a lot more sophisticated than the original. These modern high-quality cruisers use aluminum for many components; well-built, relatively light frames; and either derailleur gears, or multi-speed hub gears. The brakes can be anything from the traditional coaster brake, operated by pedaling back, to modern rim brakes borrowed from the mountain bike.

Utility Bikes

In the mid-1990s, Shimano, the major manufacturer of bicycle components, decreed (probably correctly) that the world was waiting for a different kind of bike, a bike that would be suitable for everyday transportation, requires little maintenance and finicky operator awareness. They boosted the concept of this kind of bike, the new utility bike, by introducing component groups specifically designed for that kind of use, first centered around internal hub gearing and hub brakes, now mainly with derailleur gears. In addition, they sponsored competitions for the most innovative use of those products in new bike designs.

So far, not many of the real utilitarian results have hit the American market (unlike in Europe, where they are embraced by many major manufacturers and the cycling public). Specialized and Bianchi introduced elegant Italian-built bikes based on this concept, and Wheeler brings in some models from Japan. My guess is that it will perhaps take a few years, but eventually there'll be plenty of choice.

A good utility bike should be suitable for riding and carrying things under all conditions, including rain and snow. That means not only racks and fenders, but also an enclosed chainguard (to allow you to ride it with regular street wear), generator lights (so you can count on having lights available even if you weren't planning on riding in the dark), internal hub gears, and internal hub brakes (both of which work in any kind of weather). Count on spending $600 or more for a good multi-speed utility bike.

Roadsters and Three-Speeds

Although still available in Britain, they don't bring them into the U.S. anymore. Roadsters first entered the U.S. market under the guise of "English Racers" in the early fifties, because they seemed like racers when compared to the 45-pound bikes most Americans were riding at the time. But in the U.S., these bikes have virtually disappeared from the bike trade by now.

If you like the simplicity and upright posture they offer, as well as some of the same virtues that are on my wish list for the ultimate utility bike, look at garage sales and bike swaps—lots of those machines with Sturmey-Archer three-speed hubs, elegant fenders, and upright handlebars are being sold for peanuts. A little attention will turn most of them into very serviceable machines. (See Chapter 6 to learn more about buying a used bike.)

Fig. 2.6. Typical modern cruiser. This Street Rod model from Electra Cycles is styled after the Schwinn cantilever frame-bikes but comes with Shimano's four-speed internal hub gearing.

BMX and Trials Bikes

Running on 20-inch diameter fat-tire wheels, BMX bikes were the first modern bikes intended for off-road cycling, making them precursors to the current mountain bike craze. They are used to best effect on special courses and are less suitable for longer bike rides. Some of the technology for competition-level BMX bikes is quite sophisticated and has rubbed off on the mountain bike.

The 24-inch wheel equivalent of the BMX bike is referred to as either cruisers (not to be confused with the more common 26-inch cruisers) or dirt bikes. They also have knobby tires.

Trials bikes are also derived from the same stock, and are typically 24-inch-wheel machines with small frames that are particularly suited to doing tricks.

Cyclo-Cross Bikes

Cyclo-cross is the original off-road form of bicycle racing, which preceded mountain biking by some 60 years. A cyclo-cross bike looks like a road bike. It has relatively narrow knobby tires and drop handlebars. But the gearing is similar to the wide range gearing of the mountain bike, and the same cantilever brakes are used that were installed on early mountain bikes. The cyclo-cross bike is a lovely lightweight alternative to the mountain bike for off-road riding, but it is much more fragile and not as easy to ride. Expect to pay at least $1,000 for this kind of bike.

Fixed-Wheel Bikes

The fixed-wheel bike looks like a road bike, but instead of derailleur gearing it has a directly driven rear wheel. No freewheel, no gears. Traditionally used for bicycle track racing, this ultimately simple machine has recently been rediscovered for urban use, primarily by bike messengers. Because you can't stop pedaling when going around a corner, it's important that the frame be designed specifically for this kind of drive. Fun to ride, beautifully simple and straightforward, good practice for developing a smooth riding style, but torture on steep hills. Expect to pay at least $600 for anything worthy of the name.

The difference between a regular track racing bike and a "street fixed-wheel bike" is that the former does not have a brake, while the one you might want to use on the road should at least have a front brake. In the rear, just trying to restrain the pedals will give all the braking effect you can expect there.

Folding Bikes

The idea of reducing a bicycle to a package compact enough for transportation is almost as old as the bicycle itself. In recent years, responding in part to the restrictive policies for carrying bikes on planes and other forms of public transport, many innovations have come to market. It's worth considering if you travel a lot and find a use for a bicycle wherever you go. Good folding bikes start at about $600, but you can pay as much as $5,000 for a top-of-the-line Alex Moulton.

Folding bikes fall into several different categories, although most are considered utility bikes. There are folders with skinny tires that behave like road bikes, and there are those with fat tires that feel like mountain bikes—some of them with front and rear suspension. There are even folding tandems—an engineering challenge if ever there was one, due to the high forces working on a tandem frame.

Perhaps the most common, though rather marginal, folding bike in the U.S. is the DaHon—it folds very ingeniously, but it suffers from the restraints placed upon the design by the manufacturer's pricing policy: cheap sort of precludes good.

Fig. 2.7. Modern lightweight folding bike. This Birdie by Burley rides like a full-size bike, thanks to its sophisticated full-suspension system.

Green Gear Cycling of Eugene, Oregon, makes a series of high-quality folding machines under the name BikeFriday, while its neighbor Burley, best known for its tandems, markets a German design called Birdie. Other folding and collapsible machines include the famous Alex Moulton small-wheeled suspension bikes, and the very ingenious and simple Brompton, also from England. The Montague bikes are a case apart; they are full-size bikes, with regular size wheels, that fold compactly. A few other rather sophisticated full-size bikes are much like it in that they can be taken apart with the use of special connecting fittings in the main tubes, allowing the bike to fit in a compact carrying case.

Tandems

There has been a resurgence of tandems—bicycles built for two—during the last ten years or so. Road and mountain bike versions are available. There are even track-racing tandems and recumbent tandems. The tandem's advantages are that it keeps riders of different skill levels together, and that it travels faster than a single bike, especially against the wind. On the down side, all tandems are heavy, cumbersome, and expensive. The equivalent tandem to a $600 road or mountain bike will weigh

Fig. 2.8. Modern road tandem. This is the author's custom-built tandem, based on a frame of his own design, built by California frame builder Bernie Mikkelsen.

40 pounds and cost $1,500, and it seems the sky is the limit for the price of upscale models.

Braking is a big problem on most tandems, certainly when going downhill fast. It's advisable to practice a lot to learn about the limitations of braking effectiveness at speed before taking the tandem out on a serious ride. Other aspects of tandem riding also should be practiced, because this long and somewhat cumbersome machine acts differently from the bike you're used to, not to mention the need for the two partners to learn to work together and coordinate their efforts.

When buying a tandem, take your prospective partner along. That way, you can select a bike that both of you like, and both of you benefit from the instructions given at the bike shop.

Recumbents and Hand Cycles

This is an entirely different category of cycles (both bicycles and tricycles can fall into this category). Recumbents differ from the conventional bicycle in that the rider sits leaning back with his or her legs pointing forward rather than dangling down. There are many different models, but very few of them are available at regular bike stores. Their prices start at about $1,000 for a bike that performs well, and are virtually open-ended at the top.

On some recumbents, you can install fairings that keep the rider dry in bad weather and improve aerodynamic performance. Although they can be rather cumbersome due to their often great length, they can be a great solution for people who find conventional bikes uncomfortable. They also may have a safety edge because the rider's low mass center and the long wheelbase prevent most mechanisms that lead to dangerous falls.

Hand cycles are usually set up like recumbents, but are propelled by hand-cranking instead of being pedal-driven. They allow people with lower body disabilities to keep up with others on the road. Although you won't find many shops that stock hand cycles (or recumbents for that matter), they should have the information available to special-order one for you.

3

Understanding the Bicycle

IN THIS CHAPTER, we'll take a look at what all bikes have in common, and define how the various parts differ for different types of machines. Figure 3.1 on page 30 depicts a simple mountain bike, labeled with the names of the various parts.

The Parts of the Bike

A bike consists of a frame and a number of components that are installed on the frame. The bicycle manufacturer assembles those parts to the finished frame. Some of the other parts, such as the wheels, themselves consist of a number of smaller separate components that have been assembled before they are installed on the bike.

The various components come from specialized manufacturers. A lot of those parts are supplied by one of a small number of manufacturers of bicycle components. Among those, Shimano is the biggest and most common. This Japanese manufacturer produces whole series of components in many different price and quality categories. A complete package of parts is referred to as a "gruppo" in the U.S., or "group-set" in Britain.

Although everything Shimano makes works quite well, it's not necessarily an indication of a particular quality level if a bike is referred to as "Shimano-equipped." Your question should be,

"What quality are those Shimano components?" There are
Shimano-made component groups used on the $100 cash-and-
carry bike from a discount store, as well as on a $3,000 custom
bike, and obviously they're not the same.

On average, about one half of the total cost of a bike goes
into the frame, the other half into the components. Consequently,
you can assume that the components mounted on the $100 bike
are worth only about $50, while $1,500 worth of components

*Fig. 3.1. The parts of the bicycle, showing the names for the various
components as used in this book.*

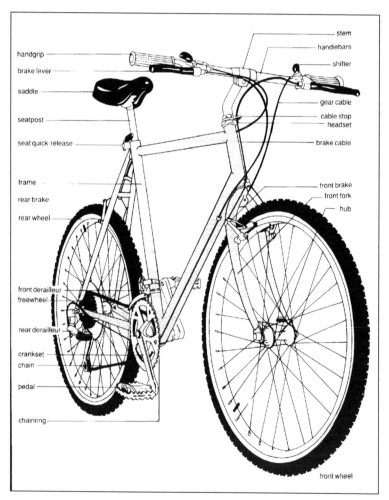

may have been installed on the $3,000 marvel in the window of the upscale bike shop.

The various components can be broken down on the basis of the functional groups they constitute. Besides the frame itself, those are the steering system, the wheels, the brakes, the drivetrain, the gearing system, the seat, and other components (which on many mountain bikes include suspension components).

The Frame

The conventional bicycle frame is built using tubes that are connected together to form a rigid structure. In addition to the conventional materials of steel and aluminum, other materials, such as titanium, metal matrix, and carbon fiber, are being used increasingly. Unconventional designs are made possible through the use of carbon fiber and similar materials. These are mainly used on high-end mountain bikes, where the use of complex suspension systems creates the incentive to move away from the traditional and familiar diamond-shaped frame design; they are also used on high-end road bikes.

Each of these materials can be made into a light and strong frame. Indeed some steel frames are lighter than many aluminum or carbon fiber frames, and some aluminum frames are as strong as any steel frame. It depends on the type of steel or other material used and how it is assembled. If you hear a bike is made of "chrome-moly" (sometimes shortened to "cro-mo"), that's not some magic metal, but one of several types of steel that are suitable for strong and reasonably light frames. The highest quality metal tubing, both steel and aluminum, are butted, meaning that the tubes have thinner walls in the middle than at the ends. This makes for a lighter frame.

The various parts of the conventional frame are categorized as main frame and rear triangle. The thick tubes of the main frame are head tube, top tube, downtube and seat tube. The rear triangle consists of pairs of thinner pairs of tubes, called seat stays and chain stays. The bottom bracket is the point at the bottom of the seat tube where it is connected with the downbube and the chain stays. This is where the bottom bracket (the bearings and spindle for the cranks) is installed. At the top, the rear triangle's seat stays are attached to the seat tube just below the seat lug, which is the part where the seatpost is clamped in.

The most important criterion for the frame is that it must be the right size to match the rider, and that subject will be covered extensively in Chapter 4, "Sizing Your Bike." The other aspect to consider is that different kinds of bikes have different frame designs. For example, mountain bikes are not just road bikes with fatter tires, but also call for a specific frame design.

The Steering System

The components that make the bike steer are referred to as the steering system. It consists of the front fork, held in the frame's head tube by means of a set of bearings called the headset, and the handlebars with the stem that connects them to the fork. Again, these components differ as a function of the bike's use. For example, road bikes have drop handlebars, while mountain bikes typically have straight, flat handlebars and often suspension forks.

The Wheels

After the frame, the wheels are the main items that characterize a specific type of bike. Fat 26-inch wheels for mountain bikes, skinny 700 mm wheels (nominally 700 mm is about 28 inches, but their actual outside diameter is about 27 inches) for road bikes, slightly fatter ones for hybrids and touring bikes, small ones for folding bikes, and so on.

Each wheel consists of a rim on which the tire and the inner tube are mounted, a hub with bearings around which the wheel rotates, and a set of spokes to tie it all together. The lighter the wheel, the nimbler the ride; the fatter the tires, the better their shock-absorption qualities.

The Brakes

Depending on what type of bike you've got, the brakes are somewhat different. On mountain bikes direct-pull brakes (also referred to as V-brakes) are commonly used today. Older mountain bikes, as well as most hybrids, touring bikes, tandems, and cyclo-cross bikes use cantilever brakes. Both types are mounted on bosses (metal attachments with pivot points) permanently installed on the seatstays and the front fork.

Road bikes generally use sidepull brakes, which are installed as complete units to the front fork, and a bridge piece between the seatstays of the frame. In addition, there are brakes built into the hub, as used on the old cruiser and some of the newer incarnations of the utility bike that are just now being introduced, and as disk brakes on downhill-type mountain bikes.

The brakes are operated by means of levers mounted on the handlebars (except coaster brakes, which are operated simply by pedaling back). Again, the type of levers varies with the type of bike, and those for high-end road bikes nowadays are usually integrated with the shift lever mechanism for the gears, and are suitable only for use with drop handlebars. On mountain bikes, the brake levers are specifically designed for use with the mountain bike's flat handlebars.

The brake levers are connected with the brake mechanisms by means of flexible control cables (unless they are operated hydraulically, as is the case on some downhill-type mountain bikes).

Left: Fig. 3.2. Steering system on a mountain bike with front suspension.

Below: Fig. 3.3. Drivetrain and gearing on a mountain bike.

The Drivetrain

The drivetrain is the set of components that transmits your leg motion to the rear wheel. Although the gearing system components are sometimes considered part of the drivetrain too, I will treat those separately below.

The cranks are attached to the bottom bracket spindle that runs on bearings in the frame's bottom bracket (sometimes called "BB" for short). Chainrings of different sizes are attached to the right crank, and the pedals are screwed onto the ends of the crankarms. Upscale pedals are clipless, meaning— paradoxically—that they clip onto special shoes, whereas simpler bikes have pedals that can be ridden with any shoes.

The other parts of the drivetrain are the chain and the cogs on the rear wheel's hub, as well as the freewheel mechanism on which the cogs are mounted.

The Gearing System

Except for some recently introduced utility bikes and old-style cruisers (and, in England, three-speed roadsters), modern bikes have derailleur gearing. This system simply shoves the chain sideways from one combination of front chainring and rear cog to another. Since the differences are in the number of teeth on chainring and cog respectively, the result is that the same pedaling speed is translated into a higher or lower rotating speed for the rear wheel. The theory and practice will be explained in Chapter 8, "Using the Gears."

The rear derailleur is mounted to the right of the rear wheel hub and is controlled from a shifter on the right side of the handlebars. The front derailleur is mounted to the right of the frame's seat tube, just above the chainrings, and it is controlled from a shifter on the left side of the handlebars.

The type of shifter depends on the type of bike. On most mountain bikes, they are mounted under the handgrips, or sometimes a twistgrip is used, on which the shifting mechanism is combined with the handgrip. On hybrids, twistgrips are used most frequently. On high-end road bikes, the shifters are usually integrated with the brake levers. On touring bikes and some road bikes, the shifters may be either on the ends of the drop handlebars or on the side of the frame's downtube. The new crop of internal-hub–geared utility bikes uses either a single twistgrip or a shift lever mounted under the handlebars. Whatever type, the shifters are connected with the matching mechanism by means of a flexible cable similar to that used to control the brakes.

The Saddle

Also referred to as the seat, the saddle is attached to the frame by means of the seatpost, which is clamped into the frame's seat lug. The height can be varied by loosening this connection and tightening it again at a different point. However, it's critically important that the seatpost should never be raised so far that it is not clamped in securely. For that reason, the seatpost should have a minimum-insertion mark on the seatpost. If the seat cannot be raised adequately without exposing this mark, the frame is probably too small for you, and the safest solution is to get a bike with a bigger frame.

Other Parts

Mountain bikes often have suspension forks in the front and may have some other suspension mechanism built into the frame for the rear wheel. Other components that may be installed on some bikes include racks (called carriers in Britain) for carrying luggage; lights and reflectors to enable safe night riding; fenders (called mudguards in Britain) to fend off water and mud; cyclo computers to keep track of your speed and distance travelled; and warning devices to help you get noticed.

Except for suspension components, which usually are designed as integral parts of the bike, most of the other accessories listed here are mainly sold as aftermarket items.

Know Your Gruppos

These days, bikes are usually equipped with a gruppo (a set of components) rather than the grab-bag of components from different manufacturers that was quite typical in the days of the ten-speed and the early days of mountain biking. The particular gruppo installed says a lot about the quality of the bike. In this section, we'll take a look at some of the gruppos found on bicycles and what they mean in terms of price and quality.

Often a bike is not really equipped with a complete gruppo. Instead, the bicycle's manufacturer or importer may have gone for the appeal of a higher-end gruppo but saved some money by substituting cheaper parts for the less obvious ones. This is often a good way to keep the price down. That does not necessarily result in an inferior bike. For example, some non-Shimano brakes and cranksets may be at least as good as Shimano's equivalents offered as part of a certain gruppo. The rear derailleur is generally considered the telltale part of a gruppo, and it's easy enough to put on a rear derailleur from a high-end gruppo, but many of the other components, such as front derailleur, crankset, brakes, pedals, and headset, may be from a lower-quality gruppo. That may fool you into thinking you're getting the level of quality associated with the glamorous rear derailleur, when in fact you are not.

Mountain Bike Gruppos

Ever since the demise of SunTour in the early 1990s, it's been almost all Shimano in mountain biking. Besides Shimano, SRAM and its subsidiary, Sachs, offer fine products as well. Here's the Shimano mountain bike gruppo lineup from top to bottom.

XTR (precise and lightweight, found only on the most expensive bikes intended mainly for competition costing $1,500 or more)

Deore XT (excellent quality but some parts slightly heavier; installed mainly on high-end bikes costing $800 or more)

Deore LX (good quality but slightly heavier again; found on bikes costing $600 or more)

STX-RC (OK quality; found mainly on nice recreational-level bikes)

Alevio (recreational-level equipment with cantilever brakes instead of direct-pull brakes)

Acera, Altus, Tourney, CX, MJ (work fine when new but have adjustability and wear problems; MJ is sized for young teenagers)

Nexus, Nexave (designed for city bikes and utility bikes, works very well for the purpose and is mentioned at the end of this list only because it is different, not because it's cheaper than recreational-level mountain bike gruppos)

Road Bike Gruppos

In this category, Campagnolo is still a viable alternative to Shimano's products. Other manufacturers, mainly Sachs and Mavic, are also factors here. Here are the lineups for Shimano and Campagnolo respectively, again listed from top to bottom.

Shimano Road Gruppos

Dura-Ace (Shimano's finest; used for high-end competition bikes costing $1,500 or more)

Ultegra (slightly heavier and less polished, but excellent quality; used on bikes costing $800 or more)

105 SC (OK quality when new, but with more plastic and slightly more susceptible to wear and damage; used on bikes costing $600 or more)

RX 100, RSX, Exage 300 EX (work fine when new but have adjustability and wear problems)

Campagnolo Road Gruppos

Record (the choice of champions and others who can afford it, used on bikes costing $1,500 or more)

Chorus (almost as nice but less titanium—at a substantial savings; used on bikes costing $1,000 or more)

Athena (good enough for most racing and long, fast riding; used on bikes costing $800 or more)

Veloce (in the same price category as Shimano's 105 but nicer finish and more durable; used on bikes costing $600 or more)

Mirage, Avanti (good value for recreational-level road bikes)

Speed TH (special equipment for high-end triathlon bikes with 26-inch wheels; listed at the end of this list only because it's different, while it fits in the same category as Record equipment)

4

Sizing Your Bike

SIZE MATTERS on a bicycle. Although you *can* probably ride almost any size bike, you'll be amazed at the increase in comfort, speed, and safety achieved when you get a bike that's sized just right for you. We'll look at three aspects of the sizing equation: fixed dimensions, adjustable ones, and modifiable ones.

Fixed dimensions are those that are given for the particular bike, like the size of the frame and the wheels. Adjustable ones are features such as the height and angle of the saddle and the handlebars—things that can be adjusted to make a given bike more fitting to its rider. Modifiable dimensions are those that can only be changed by replacing a part by one of a different size.

Some dimensions are limited by factors of design for any given kind of bicycle. Mountain bikes, for example, come with 26-inch tires, and to accommodate that wheel size, other dimensions of the frame are also bound to certain maxima and minima. Just the same, that still allows frames to be constructed that fit all but the very smallest and tallest riders. That's why mountain bikes are available in a number of different frame sizes. You'll be most comfortable selecting one that's designed for riders of approximately your size.

Some bike shops have special devices for sizing a bike to the customer's physique. Although it is best to use those devices, when available, under the guidance of the bike shop personnel, it's also important to understand the criteria yourself, and that's what the rest of this chapter is about.

Frame Size

There are a number of different ways to define the size of the
frame, as illustrated in Fig. 4.1. For mountain bikes and hybrids
the frame size is usually given in inches, whereas road bike
frames are measured in cm (centimeters—one cm equals
0.4 inches).

Manufacturers' catalogues usually define the bike's size
by the length of the seat tube. This is measured from the center
of the bottom bracket either to the center of the top tube or to the
top of the seat lug. The difference between these two methods is
the distance from the center of the top tube to the top of the seat
lug, as measured along the center of the seat tube. On models
with a lowered or missing top tube (such as those that are used,
for example, on "ladies" models and folding bikes), frame size is
always measured to the top of the seat lug.

Another way of defining frame size is by the straddle height
(also called stand-over height). This is the height of the top of the
top tube above the ground. On models with a sloping top tube, it
is measured at a point just in front of the saddle.

The relationship between frame sizes measured by the seat
tube length and those measured by the straddle height is not the
same for all frames, because the height of the bottom bracket
above the ground may differ and the angle of the seat tube
varies. On mountain bikes, the bottom bracket is usually higher

Fig. 4.1. Frame size and other characteristic dimensions, also showing a
definition of the rider's inseam measurement as used for sizing the frame.

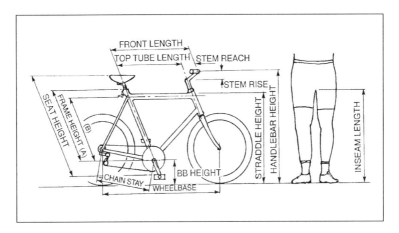

than on other machines, so there a given seat tube length results in a greater straddle height than it does on a road bike.

Probably the most critical dimension is the straddle height. You have to be able to straddle the top tube comfortably to be safe on the bike. Consequently, it should be at least an inch less than your inseam leg length. Test it by standing across the top tube just in front of the saddle: it's the right size if you can raise the front wheel by about 5 to 6 inches for a mountain bike, or 3 inches for a road bike, hybrid, touring bike, or any other conventional bicycle.

Be careful if the bike has a lowered or missing top tube. In this case, you'll have plenty of straddle height even on a bike that is otherwise too big. On machines like this, the minimum saddle height is a more critical dimension. You should be able to reach the ground with both feet when the saddle is in the lowest position. It's too big if you can't comfortably stand on the front of your feet, with the heels raised, too small if you have to bend your knees to have the feet flat on the ground.

What's Your Frame Size?

To give you a rough idea of the nominal frame size range to look for, use the following method. Mark the height of your crotch above the ground, standing against a wall without shoes. Measure the distance in inches between the ground and the marker, and call that dimension X. Look for a frame size determined in the following table, depending on the method of frame size designation:

Bike Type	Center-to-Center	Center-to-Top	Straddle Height
Mountain Bike	X – 14 inches	X – 12½ inches	X – 3 inches
Hybrid	X – 13 inches	X – 11½ inches	X – 2 inches
Road Bike	2.5 (X – 13) cm	2.5 (X – 11) cm	X – 1½ inches

That's the size you should look at first, but don't take it as gospel. Once you're in the bike shop and have checked out some frames in the appropriate size, make a note of what works best, and continue looking for bikes of that size. What also matters is the frame length, measured as the length of the top tube between the center of the seat tube and the center of the headtube. The manufacturers give the bikes with longer seat tubes longer top tubes as well. That's fine if you have standard proportions, but if for example, your upper body is short in comparison to your legs, you may not be comfortable on a bike with the "right" seat tube length because its top tube may be too long for you.

Saddle Height

This is the dimension defined by the fixed frame size and the extent to which the saddle is raised above the top of the seat tube. To be comfortable, the saddle should be raised to the point where you can just reach the pedals with the knee almost fully stretched, with the heel of a flat-soled shoe while sitting on the saddle. Get someone to hold you while sitting like that and pedaling back. If you can do that without rocking side-to-side, the saddle is at the right height.

To be safe, the seatpost should be clamped in over at least 2½ inches, or 65 mm. Most seatpost are engraved to show the minimum insertion height. Don't ride a bike with the saddle so high that this marker shows. If you selected the right size frame, you should never run into this problem. Since there are other criteria, such as your weight distribution over the front and the rear of the bike, it is not a good idea to "fix" a frame that's too short by using an extra long seatpost. Use only the seatpost that came with the bike, or one of the same length.

Handlebar Height

To ride comfortably in the long run, the highest point of the handlebars should be no higher than the top of the saddle. Racers put their handlebars even lower, while on utility bikes, used for short distances in an urban environment, many riders prefer the handlebars a little higher. (Of course, recumbent bikes answer to a different piper altogether).

Never raise the handlebar stem so far that it is clamped in by less than 65 mm (2½ inches) below the top of the headset. Failure of this connection is likely to lead to complete and sudden loss of control over the bike, and often causes a fall resulting in serious injuries.

Although traditionally handlebar height has been an easily variable dimension, it is no longer so, especially with modern mountain bikes. This is due to the use of a headset referred to as "Aheadset," which puts the handlebars in a fixed position. Here the only way you can change the effective handlebar height is by replacing the handlebar stem, or by choosing a different handlebar design. Even if the bike has a conventional headset, the preferred method of handlebar height adjustment is to get a stem that has the requisite rise rather than raising it.

Front Length

This is the horizontal distance between the saddle and the handlebars. For reasons beyond my comprehension, this is often referred to as "cockpit size" by bicycle magazine editors. The fixed point on the saddle is considered the point where a line through the center of the seatpost intersects with the top of the saddle. The fixed point on the handlebars is the handlebar's center. Clearly, this allows for some variation. The saddle can be moved back and forth by about 2 inches ("adjustable" dimension). The handlebars can be moved closer or farther out by selecting a longer or shorter stem, or you can choose a different handlebar design ("modifiable" dimensions).

The bike should be comfortable, but you'll probably find that the way it's set up at first may not be comfortable if you're a beginner. It takes some practice to get used to the rather stretched-out posture for which most modern "real" mountain and road bikes are designed (recreational bikes and hybrids tend to be significantly shorter). Besides, if you have a long or a short combination of upper body and arms, the standard configuration the way the bike came from the factory may not be suitable. Specifically, many women have this problem because their arms and upper body tend to be shorter than what is the average for most men of the same size—and that's what most manufacturers use as the basis for their frame designs.

The most elegant, but expensive, way out of this is by getting a custom-built bike frame, literally made to measure. If you can't find a bike with a short enough top tube, look into special bikes intended for women, such as those offered by a company called Terry Precision Cycling for Women.

Without resorting to special equipment, this kind of problem can often be alleviated by making adjustments and modifications to the position of both the handlebars and the saddle. To maintain your weight distribution the way the bike was designed, I recommend you don't just use a longer or shorter handlebar stem, but to "split the difference" by also moving the saddle back or forward by about the same distance. To get 2 inches more effective front length, get a stem that's about 1 inch longer, and move the saddle about 1 inch back on the seatpost.

Other Dimensions

There are three other variables that matter for your comfort, and all three can only be affected by replacing certain components ("modifiable" variables). These are the size and shape of the saddle, the size and shape of the handlebars, and the length of the cranks. It will be best to get these changes made at the time you buy the bike. That's when it's cheap and easy to exchange, and you'll be comfortable right from the start.

The saddle should be comfortable. That means it should have the right shape and be firmly flexible, not soft and broad. If you have a relatively wide pelvis (most women do), look for a saddle that is 1 or 2 inches wider in the back portion and with a shorter nose with a soft section in the middle near the front. You may find such specific women's saddles most comfortable.

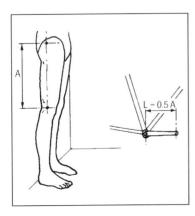

Fig. 4.2. The optimal crank length is about half the length of your thigh, as measured per this drawing.

The handlebars need to be consistent with your shoulder width. If you sit on the bike, your arms should be parallel to each other when you hold the handlebars in their normal position. The proper size for mountain bike handlebars and other flat designs is about 2 to 4 inches wider than your shoulders. Drop handlebars should be about 2 to 3 inches narrower than your shoulders for road bikes, about 1 to 2 inches narrower than your shoulders for touring bikes.

The optimal crank length is one half the length of your thigh bone, as measured per Fig. 4.2. Most manufacturers take care of that by installing slightly longer cranks on their biggest bikes, shorter ones on their smallest models. The range is quite limited. Most crank manufacturers make them in sizes 165, 170, 175, and 180 mm, a range of only 1 inch.

Although there is little risk involved in mounting shorter cranks on any given bike, there is a potential risk associated with installing longer cranks. In the first place, it brings the cranks and pedals closer to the ground when they are in their lowest position. This can be dangerous going around a curve. To prevent this risk, don't pedal through the corners (on fixed gear bicycles that is impossible because the pedals turn with the wheels, so never put longer cranks on those machines). In the second place, it brings them closer to the front wheel when they're in their forward position. That is dangerous because they may interfere with the front wheel, especially at low speeds, when the steering deviations needed to balance on the bike are much bigger than at high speeds. This, too, is critically important on fixed-wheel bikes, on which you have to continue pedaling when cornering.

5

Other Equipment for You and Your Bike

IN ADDITION to the bike itself, you will want to buy a couple of other items. They range from essential things for the protection of your bike and your person to accessories that make cycling more comfortable or more interesting. This chapter will show you what to get and how to choose the individual items you've decided to buy.

Gear for the Rider

In this first section, we'll look at the items you may want to buy for your own protection.

Helmet

If any single accessory is important, it's the bicycle helmet. If you do fall off your bike and hit your head on the pavement or against some obstacle, the helmet will most likely reduce the impact to the point where what might have been a significant injury becomes a mere scrape, and it can save your life in a serious accident.

The modern cycling helmet is remarkably light and comfortable—and effective. The main protection is offered by a

¾ inch thick layer of crushable foam material, while the exterior skin consists of a thin layer of a hard smooth plastic. In case of a fall, the foam is crushed and thereby passes on the energy absorbed in the impact slowly enough to protect the brain—or at least to significantly decrease the likelihood of serious injury. The smooth outer skin allows the helmet to skid along the surface of the road, reducing the rotational force on the neck.

All bicycle helmets sold in bike stores in the U.S., and most other countries these days, are good, though none are perfect. They reduce the impact but can't eliminate it. That applies to the cheap ones as well as the expensive ones. They all pass the same tests. The big difference in price is largely reflected in their comfort and styling: expensive helmets have more ventilation and may look more attractive.

The first step is to measure the size of your head (using a tape wrapped around your head just above the ears). With that figure, the bike shop personnel can tell you what your helmet size will be. Try on several helmets in your size that visually appeal to you—or, if you're on a tight budget, have prices you can afford. You'll find that they don't all fit the same way: some fit better on a long, relatively narrow head; others fit better on a rounder skull.

Whereas the standard helmet is designed in a variety of sizes for a typical male skull, some models are designed wider, and that often makes them more suitable for women. Women's

Fig. 5.1. A selection of bicycle helmets in a store display.

Fig. 5.2. A variety of cycling shoes in a store display.

heads tend to be wider relative to their size. But not all people are average. Consequently, a male with a smallish but wide head may be well fitted with a woman's model, and if you're a woman but have a relatively narrow head, look at a small version of a regular men's model rather than a women's.

Choose any one that feels comfortable, then make final fitting adjustments using the foam inserts provided and by readjusting the straps. The helmet should fit firmly enough so that it does not twist around on your head when you turn your head, or bob up-and-down when moving. The straps should be adjusted so that you can get about a finger thickness between your neck and the chin strap. Make sure the straps are adjusted so that the helmet can't come off and the chin strap can't slip over your chin.

Cycling Shoes

Simple bikes with conventional pedals can usually be ridden with any kind of shoes that are not too bulky and have a firm sole. But special cycling shoes—definitely needed if your bike has clipless pedals—will significantly add to your comfort.

For use with clipless pedals, the matching plates (there are several standards, such as Shimano, Look, and Ritchie) must be installed. Their position is adjustable, and they should be set so that the ball of the foot is over the pedal axle and your feet rotate naturally with the pedal revolution. Adjust the release spring force so that you can easily twist your foot out in case of a sudden need to escape.

I recommend shoes with Velcro fasteners. Many shoes have shoelaces that get covered by Velcro straps. Either solution is safer than having conventional shoelaces dangling loose, which may get caught in the chain and cause a fall.

Cycling Clothing

You can get special cycling shorts, tights, jerseys, jackets, gloves, and even socks. They are all designed with cycling in mind, and they'll improve your riding comfort. If you don't want to dress the part quite this seriously, wear clothing you already have, providing it's light, flexible, and comfortable.

Cycling shorts and gloves are padded in the area of contact with the saddle and the handlebars respectively. The padding significantly increases comfort on longer rides. Especially with gloves this is important, because it prevents injury to the nerve endings in the palms of the hand.

The most comfortable material for cycle clothing is wool, especially if it's been enhanced by blending it with a small percentage of a highly elastic synthetic material that keeps its shape better, such as spandex (also known as Lycra).

Rain Gear

If you live in a part of the world where the weather is not sufficiently predictable to always stay dry (or if you're serious enough about cycling to do it even if the weather is not perfect), at least get a rain jacket. It should close with a generous flap in the front, and it should be long enough in the back to cover your rear when you're bent over in the saddle. Rain pants and even rain booties are also available, but they may be more hassle than they're worth.

Sunglasses and Sunblock

If you're out for a protracted time in sunny weather, I recommend you use both sunglasses and sunblock. I don't think there is ever any justification to get a sunscreen lotion with less than the highest available protection factor. In addition to sunglasses, I suggest a visor that clips to the helmet, to reduce the blinding effect of a low sun.

Gear for the Bike

In this section, we'll consider the products to buy that can be considered tools and accessories for the bicycle. First, a word of warning concerning any gadgets you may want to install on the bike. Make sure they're attached firmly, and check their attachments regularly. Accessories that come loose sometimes cause grave danger. To give just one example, there have been a number of very serious accidents caused by loose front fenders.

If the mounting stays come loose, the whole thing can finish up caught in the front wheel, bringing the bike to a sudden stop and pitching the rider over the front—head first. Avoid things like that by remaining alert to the condition of the bike and its accessories, and getting them fixed immediately.

Bar-Ends

Bar-ends are installed at the ends of flat mountain bike handlebars to make them more comfortable and versatile. Adjust them so that they project forward, pointing up by only about 10 to 15 degrees.

Lock

Get a lock to improve your chances of keeping your bike for a long time. The popular U-shaped locks—certainly those made by Kryptonite—are a good choice, but large-diameter cable locks from the same manufacturer are more versatile and harder to crack. Don't just lock the bike by itself but to something immovable. It's best to take the front wheel out and lock it up with the rear portion of the bike. If your bike has a seat with a quick-release, you may even have to remove it, and either lock it as well or take it along with you. The same goes for anything else that's not solidly anchored on the bike: remove things such as lights, bags, and cyclo computer.

Water Bottle

Bicycle water bottles are mounted by means of a little metal cage installed on the frame. Get at least one—two if you'll be going on longer rides in remote areas and drink frequently, especially if it's hot and you're exerting yourself. Another solution is a hydration system worn on the back, such as the Camelbak.

Pump

You'll need at least a small pump that can be carried on the bike, and preferably a floor pump with integral pressure gauge for use at home. The small pump can either be the type that fits between the frame tubes (make sure you get a size that fits), or a "telescoping" one that literally fits in a jersey pocket. If you want to trade some money for effort (pray, why are you buying a muscle-powered bike?), you can buy an inflator using pressurized CO_2 gas cartridges.

Make a note of the pressure to which your tires should be inflated for any kind of use (more for smooth roads than for rough ones) and check them before every ride, at least on a road bike. To check the pressure, buy a small tire pressure gauge if the pump does not have a built-in gauge, but be prepared to add air each time you do, because checking the pressure always releases some air.

Lights

If your trip can possibly extend into darkness, or even just dusk, you should have lights with you. Spectacularly bright lights are now available for serious night riding. If you'll be riding in the dark only occasionally and in an urban or suburban environment, you may be adequately served with just a big rear reflector or a flashing rear light, strapped to the seatpost, and an easily removable battery-operated front light that's clipped to

Fig. 5.3. Bright cycling lights. These dual-beam high-output lights from NiteRider are typical for what is available for serious nighttime riding these days. But they are not cheap.

the handlebars. Aim the front light at a point on the road about 20 to 30 feet straight ahead of you. Don't count on front or side reflectors protecting you: reflectors are only visible to those whose headlights are aimed at them. Although that's always the case with anybody who might endanger you from the rear (assuming his or her lights are working), that's not the case with those who might run into you from ahead or the side.

Cyclo Computer

Useful for telling you not only how fast you're going but also how far and, on sophisticated models, how fast you are pedaling. That can be helpful for orientation (in combination with a map or route instructions). Most are connected with electric wiring to a sensor that is mounted on the fork, and are used together with a magnetic device that must be installed on the front wheel.

Heart Rate Monitor

If you're serious about using your bike for fitness, speed, and performance, get a heart rate monitor, or HRM. It is a wristwatch-type device with a sensor that is tied around your chest to pick up and display your heartbeat. It usually comes with an instruction manual that explains its use. You can get maximum benefit from your HRM by reading a book about it (two relevant titles are listed in the bibliography on page 95).

Bags

You may need at least a small bag to keep some items such as tools, a spare tube, and the light when not in use. Most convenient are wedge-shaped bags that fit under the back of the saddle. Carrying your stuff in a backpack is possible but gets uncomfortable, especially on longer trips. Handlebar bags are OK too, providing they are firmly held either with a clip, as provided on Cannondale bags, or with a bracket at the handlebars in combination with a bungee cord to stop the bag from swaying when you ride over bumps.

Racks

To attach heavier bags, such as for touring, you'll need to get racks installed on the bike. They're available for the front and the rear, and if you are planning on doing that, you should make sure before you buy the bike that it has the requisite hardware (bosses and eyelets) welded to the frame to mount racks. There's also a rack that can be simply clamped to the seatpost; it's adequate for a smallish bag or package.

Trailers

Another good way to carry things with the bike is by means of a trailer attached to the bike. There are two- and one-wheel models available, and the former are probably also the safest way of carrying a child.

Attachment and Removal of Accessories

Finally on this subject, some general advice. First, be aware that some accessories have a dual function, of which sometimes the secondary one turns out to be the more important one.

Consider, for example, the front reflector. Although it's of limited use (tending to lull you into believing it makes you visible to any and all riders who might run into you from in front), the bracket with which it is mounted is an essential safety

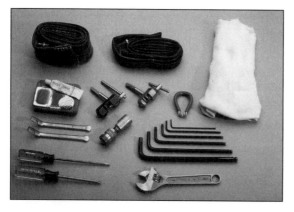

Fig. 5.4. A selection of simple bicycle tools that can be carried on the bike for a longer trip. These tools also serve well as the basis for a simple home workshop.

component on bikes with cantilever brakes. Without it, a broken or dislodged front brake cable would likely lead to the straddle cable getting caught on the tire, stopping the front wheel instantaneously and sending the rider over the handlebars. So leave that bracket there, even if you're not planning to use the front reflector (use a headlight instead).

The other aspect is that any accessory must be attached properly. If it's not, either fix it immediately or remove it altogether. Loose and broken accessories can be a hazard at worst, and at best they detract from your riding enjoyment.

Tools and Spares

You may not want to worry about things going wrong with the bike, but it will still be best to prepare for it. We'll discuss essential maintenance and basic repairs in Chapters 11 and 12 respectively. You already know to take a pump. The best way to carry the other tools is in a little pouch that can be attached to the wires of the saddle and closed tightly with a cinch strap to stop the tools from rattling.

The minimum of tools you should carry on the bike for a trip in excess of 30 minutes is the following:

❑   tire patch kit or spare tube (preferably both)

❑   set of tire levers

❑   set of Allen wrenches (2, 3, 4, 5, and 6 mm)

❑   small screwdriver

❑   cloth (to wipe your hands after working on the bike)

For longer rides (day trips) also get the following:

❑   chain tool

❑   crank bolt tool or 8 mm Allen wrench to fit crank bolt

❑   small adjustable wrench

❑   spoke wrench

Alternately, you can buy a special compact multitool, such as the Alien, that takes the place of all but the cloth and the patch kit. If you carry lights, also take spare bulbs and batteries.

6

Buying a Used Bike

ALTHOUGH MOST of what is covered in this book applies equally, regardless of whether you are buying a new bike or a used one, this chapter will deal specifically with things to consider when buying a used machine.

In today's rapidly changing bicycle market, buying used is a more viable alternative than most new cyclists realize—and some of us old hands are reaping the benefits. Like personal computer technology, the premium for the newest and latest quickly recedes under the limelight of the next hot trend to become new and wonderful. So yesterday's news is being sold off at deep discounts today. Meanwhile, what was new and wonderful last year is still pretty adequate—better in fact than what the same money can buy new today.

There is always a crop of much older bikes, such as the tenspeeds, three-speeds, and even old cruisers being cleared out of the garages of non-cyclists. If you know what you're looking for, and are able to judge its condition, you'll probably find some true bargains this way.

Before you go in pursuit of a used bike, it will be smartest to read much of the rest of this book, because most of what is discussed there is equally relevant to an old bike as to a new one. Decide on the type of bike you're looking for. But even more importantly, find out what size of bike you need. Then learn to distinguish between different quality levels, based on the construction of the frame and the components installed. Finally check the condition of the bike and its components, which we'll discuss specifically in this chapter under "Checking it Out."

Where to Buy a Used Bike

There are a number of sources for old bikes, and it pays to check out each of them—bike shops, newspaper ads, garage sales, police auctions, bike-swaps, bike club newsletters, and shops specializing in older bikes.

In general, you're probably best advised to find a bike in a resource close to the bike business. You're more likely to find a good used bike offered for sale in a bike shop or a bike club newsletter than in a junk store or the classifieds of a general newspaper, even if it's usually at a higher price.

When a customer "trades up" for a more sophisticated or more fashionable bike, the shop may take in the old bike and either sell it for the owner on consignment or sell it outright. Although obviously bike shops have to live mainly off selling new bikes, this can be good business for them, because a satisfied customer of a used bike is likely to come back for repairs, accessories, upgrades, and eventually for a new bike.

Some bicycle-related charities, such as Trips for Kids in California, have annual bike swaps where all the bikes offered have been properly assessed for their value and condition. Finally, there's even a monthly paper, *The Bicycle Trader*, devoted specifically to the buying and selling of used bikes and components (510 Frederick Street, San Francisco, CA 94117).

Bike Theft and the Secondhand Market

Unfortunately, there is a lot of bike theft, and much of it is treated in such a cavalier fashion that it's hard to make sure you're not unwittingly encouraging it by buying a stolen bike. The best way to avoid it is to steer clear of non-bike-trade sources for used bikes. Bike shops, bike clubs, cycling enthusiasts, and bicycle charities by and large make pretty sure they're not selling hot merchandise. What you find advertised in the general press or in junk shops, or by some unknown guy at the corner of the street, is not always such a safe bet.

You should still check the bike over for any apparent tampering. For instance, if there are signs that someone tried to file away or otherwise obliterate the frame number (usually under the bottom bracket), it's not a sign of great honesty.

Although the police efforts to register bikes have been well-intentioned, they're highly ineffective in dealing with professional bike theft. Virtually all those police efforts have been local, and the bike thieves trade across city limits: the bikes stolen in city A, and registered there by the local police, are shipped to city B, where the police have records only of the bikes registered there, and none showing whether a bike was stolen in some other city. If you have good reasons to suspect that a bike offered to you is stolen, you should still inform the police, explaining specifically what evidence you have.

Checking It Out

So how can you tell whether a secondhand bike is in good condition? Riding the bike will give the experienced cyclist a quick clue to its condition. The best thing to do is to take a more experienced cyclist along, preferably one who is familiar with repairing bikes as well as riding them. However, if you're not all that experienced, or if it's a type of bike you're not familiar with, you may be able to get a feel for the quality of the bike by checking some telltale details.

Fixing up an old bike can be quite a money drain. Even on a cheap bike, a pair of tires and inner tubes will set you back

Fig. 6.1. A display of used bikes outside a San Francisco bike shop. Although many shops will sell you a used bike, this store, American Cyclery, does it in a big way.

about $50, and other replacement parts are similarly much more expensive than the price of the complete bike would suggest. Thus, what seems like a bargain—"only" requiring a couple of replacement parts like tires, chain, and seat—quickly turns into a bottomless pit. Expensive bikes may be worth it, but bikes that start out cheap when new rarely justify spending money to upgrade. As an example, you can buy a complete, though junky, new department store bike for $100. Getting one of those used for $30 but then having to replace $70 worth of bits and pieces does not exactly make for a bargain.

When looking at a used bike, assuming you've established it's the right size, first check for rust. Don't buy a bike with obvious signs of rust on parts of the frame, and especially on the moving parts. It's a sign of neglect, and moving parts that have rusted will not work smoothly, even with lubrication.

Next, check for any loose, damaged or missing parts. If they're minor parts, such as handgrips or reflectors, it'll be simple and cheap to replace them. However, if parts of the pedals, the wheels, the gears or the brakes are missing, you're looking at a seriously neglected bike. That's not a good sign, because you may well be dealing with a bike that will quickly develop serious problems in service. Unless the seller is prepared to go way down in price, and you know how to correct major problems, don't buy a seriously neglected bike.

Check operation of the brakes and gears. Pull the brake lever and release it. Lift the rear wheel, turn the pedals, and change gears. If these things don't operate smoothly, you may have to replace and lubricate the cables.

Spin the wheels and check whether they run smoothly without wobbling. Put pressure on the handlebars from side to side to make sure they don't creak. Lift the front end of the bike and bounce the front wheel to make sure the headset doesn't rattle.

Finally, if you feel the bike is in reasonable shape, take it for a ride to test the gears, the brakes, and the steering in action. You may have to leave the potential seller your driver's license and a credit card, but don't buy any bike—whether new or used—without having tested it on the road. And don't buy a bike that doesn't feel right when you ride it.

7

Setting Up Your Bike

WHEN YOU BUY a new bike, it should of course be adjusted to your size at the shop. However, after a little riding, you may find that one thing or another is not set optimally for you, and although you can go back to the shop to have it readjusted, it will be better in the long run if you learn how to make such adjustments yourself. This skill is also required if you buy a secondhand bike, or if you ever lend your bike to someone else.

Let's first recall the discussion in Chapter 4 about sizing the bike, starting on page 38. Here you'll be shown how to go about the following adjustments: saddle height, forward position and tilt, and handlebar height and tilt. In addition, you'll be shown how to adjust the brake levers for the most effective operation. The subject of adjusting the gears will be treated separately in Chapter 8, starting on page 67.

Adjusting the Saddle

First make sure the top of the saddle is horizontal. Place the bike on a horizontal surface and use either a level—the air bubble must be in the middle of the gauge—or a 3-foot ruler, which you visually align with any convenient horizontal surface, such as a kitchen countertop.

Saddle Angle Adjustment

To correct the angle if the seat is not horizontal, undo the bolt (or bolts) that hold the saddle wires to the seatpost, wiggle the seat into horizontal alignment, and tighten the bolt (or bolts) again. On most modern bikes, you'll do that with an Allen wrench, while simple old bikes may require an open-ended wrench.

Saddle Height Adjustment

The correct height of the seat, as measured from the pedals, depends on your leg length. Use one of two methods to establish the correct height—either the one based on your extended leg while sitting on the bike, or the one based on a formula and your measured leg length. Most people find the first method the most convenient.

To use it, support yourself, for example, in a door opening while sitting on the bike, your heels on the pedals, wearing flat-heeled shoes. Sitting in the saddle, you should be able to pedal

Fig. 7.1. Determining the correct saddle height on the bike: pedal down, knee almost straight.

Fig. 7.2. Multiply your inseam leg length by 1.09 to determine the saddle height by the "109% rule."

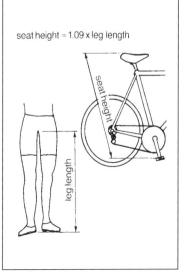

back (assuming the bike has a freewheel—you'll have to actually ride the bike, pedaling forward, if it has either a coaster brake or a fixed wheel) without having to rock sideways, yet straightening the knee almost completely as shown in Fig. 7.1. If necessary, raise or lower the saddle.

To use the second method, first measure your inseam leg length as shown in Fig 7.2. Make a note of the height of your crotch above the floor without shoes on. Multiply this figure by 1.09. This will give you the distance between the center of the bottom bracket and the top of the saddle. Although it works well for most situations, it looks more scientific than it probably is: for example, it doesn't take into account the effect of different crank lengths.

Whatever method you use, the ultimate measure will be your comfort. Use the position found this way for a couple of weeks, or at least 200 miles of riding, then be guided by your comfort to decide whether to raise or lower your seat a little (do that in steps of about ¼ inch at a time—no need to split hairs with millimeters).

To raise or lower the saddle, first undo the clamp that holds the seatpost in the frame's seat lug by loosening the binder bolt. On mountain bikes, this clamp is held with a quick-release binder bolt, while on other bikes it's simply a bolt with a nut at the other end (nowadays usually an Allen bolt, so you'll need a matching Allen wrench to loosen or tighten it). Don't under any circumstance raise the saddle so high that the maximum extension marker on the seatpost is exposed; at least 65 mm (2½ inches) of the seatpost must be clamped in below the top of the seat lug.

Saddle Quick-Release Operation

To operate a quick-release binder bolt, used on most mountain bikes, twist the lever from the "closed" to the "open" position. It should now be loose enough to move the seatpost up or down in a twisting motion.

When the seat is at the desired height and straight, tighten the quick-release by flipping the lever into the closed position. Check to make sure it is actually tightly locked in place—if it's not, first flip it back open, tighten the thumbnut on the other side by one turn, and flip it closed again (repeat if necessary).

Saddle Forward Position

You'll probably be comfortable with the saddle positioned so that the seatpost is about in the middle of the saddle. However, you may want to move it further back or forward for comfort. Generally, it is recommended (on most models other than recumbents) to have the knee joint vertically aligned with the center of the pedal spindle when the crank is in the horizontally forward position, as shown in the illustration.

To make adjustments, undo the clip bolt (or bolts) under the saddle by which the saddle's wires are held to the seatpost. Then slide the saddle back or forth, and tighten the bolt (or bolts) again, while holding the saddle horizontally and in the desired location.

Handlebar Adjustment

The safest way to adjust the handlebar height is by choosing a stem that has the right amount of rise while being clamped in all the way. On bikes with a conventional threaded headset, the height of the handlebars can also be varied by raising or lowering the handlebar stem, but it's safest to avoid raising it by more than about an inch, leaving at least 65 mm (2½ inches) clamped in. On bikes with an Aheadset, it can only be achieved by replacing the stem by one with more or less rise. Since the height of the handlebars is largely a function of rider experience, I therefore prefer conventional headsets for novice riders.

For all bikes except recumbents, the optimal handlebar height, measured at the highest point of the handlebars, is no higher than the height of the saddle, measured from the ground. Just how much lower than the seat is a matter of comfort and experience, but this gives you a starting point.

To adjust the handlebar height on a bike with a conventional headset, loosen the stem binder bolt in the top of the stem by three or four turns. If the stem does not come loose by itself, tap on the top of the bolt with a hammer to loosen it. Then move the stem up or down in a twisting motion until the handlebars are straight and as high as you want them, providing the maximum height marker on the stem does not show (the stem must be held inside the fork's steerer tube by at least 2½ inches). Tighten the expander bolt again, holding the handlebars in this position.

Check to make sure it's straight and tight by clamping the front wheel between your legs while trying to twist the handlebars—you should not be able to twist them except with great force.

On a bike with an Aheadset, the only way to change the handlebar height would be to install spacers under the stem or to find a stem with more rise. These are things you should leave to a bike shop mechanic if you are not familiar with this work.

Handlebar Angle Adjustment

Like the saddle, the handlebars can be rotated to some extent. On bikes with drop handlebars (road bikes and touring bikes) the angle can seriously affect your comfort. Here the principle is that the lower the handlebars, the more nearly horizontal the handlebar ends should be. If you keep the top of your handlebars as high as the saddle, as you might do on a touring bike, the handlebar ends may point down by about 10 degrees. A racer with really low handlebars, on the other hand, will want them perfectly horizontal.

To adjust the angle, loosen the binder bolt (or two bolts on some bikes) with which the stem's collar is clamped around the handlebars. Twist the handlebars in the desired orientation, keeping them centered. Then tighten the binder bolt or bolts.

Fig. 7.3. Relaxed posture for handlebar height and reach adjustment. The angle of your arms relative to your upper body should be about 90 degrees. Hold mountain bike bars on the bar-ends.

Brake and Gear Lever Adjustments

After you've finished putting the handlebars in the position you
find most comfortable, you may find that the brake levers are no
longer in a position that's easy to reach. To make the necessary
correction, look for the screw that clamps the lever's housing to
the handlebars. On mountain bikes and hybrids, this is usually
easy enough to find, but on drop-handlebar bikes you may have
to refer to a more detailed bike maintenance book, such as my
Road Bike Maintenance—or get it taken care of at a bike shop.

Remove and Install Wheel

You'll need to know how to remove and install the wheel,
whether it is to carry your bike in or on a car, or to fix a flat.
Since quite a few accidents have happened due to incorrect
handling of that seemingly simple process, here are detailed
instructions.

   To transport the bike, you'll usually remove the front wheel
only, but if you have to fix a flat, it's at least as likely to be the
rear wheel. Most modern bike wheels are held in with quick-
releases.

Tools and Equipment:

Usually none required

Procedure:

1. If it's the rear wheel, first place the chain on the smallest cog
   and small chainring with the derailleurs, while turning the
   cranks forward with the wheel lifted off the ground.

2. Release tension of the brake cable, either by means of the
   brake's quick-release (on a road bike with sidepull brakes)
   or by lifting out the cable (on a bike with cantilever or
   direct-pull brake).

3. Move the quick-release lever into the "open" position, and
   only loosen the thumb nut at the other end if the wheel does
   not come free. On most front forks, there are retainer tags at
   the ends of the fork that stop you from getting the wheel out
   at this point. To overcome them, loosen the thumbnut until

the quick-release is open wide enough to slip over them. The idea of these ridges is to safeguard you against the wheel from falling out if the quick-release is not tightened properly.

4. On a rear wheel, twist back the derailleur for the chain to clear the cogs as shown in Fig. 7.6.

5. Raise the bike (unless it's held upside-down), and remove the wheel.

6. To install, proceed in reverse order. On a rear wheel, hold back the rear derailleur to allow the wheel to return to its proper position and the chain to wrap around the cog and the derailleur. On a front wheel, your fight with the retainer tabs will start again: make sure the quick-release is opened far enough to fit over those tabs.

Left: Fig. 7.4. Quick-release detail. It's not tight unless you notice resistance just before you feel it snap into the "closed" position. If necessary, tighten the locknut first.

Bottom left: Fig. 7.5. Releasing cable at direct-pull brake. When reinstalling, make sure the spring end is hooked in at the brake arm.

Below: Fig. 7.6. Holding back the derailleur for wheel removal and installation. Note the chain routing.

7. Put the quick-release lever is in the "open" position, and hold the wheel exactly aligned in the center between the fork blades or stays. Tension the quick-release by twisting the lever to the "closed" position (but first retighten the thumb nut if you had to loosen it under point 3 above).

8. Check to make sure the wheel is all the way in to the end of the slots in the fork or the rear dropouts, and that it is held firmly with the quick-release lever in the "closed" position.

9. Retension the brake, and make any other adjustments that may be necessary.

Remove and Install Pedals

That's a job you may have to do when transporting a bike, especially if you're not carrying it on a roofrack but in a box.

Tools and Equipment:

❑ pedal wrench (a long, skinny open-ended wrench) or long-handled Allen wrench

❑ cloth and preferably some grease

Removal Procedure:

1. Place the pedal wrench on the stub between the right pedal and the crank (the right crank is the one with the chainrings), or the Allen wrench in the recess in the pedal's threaded stub, reached from behind the crank.

2. To unscrew the right pedal, turn the wrench counterclockwise ("to the left") as seen from the pedal side, restraining at the crank.

3. To unscrew the left pedal (which has a left-hand screw thread), turn the wrench clockwise ("to the right") as seen from the pedal, again restraining at the crank.

Installation Procedure:

1. Clean both the screw-threaded hole in the crank and the pedal's threaded stub thoroughly and lightly apply grease.

Fig. 7.7. Installing pedal using a pedal wrench. Hold the crank for leverage.

Fig. 7.8. If you grease the pedal stub, you can remove and install it with an Allen wrench.

2. Establish which is the right pedal—it is usually marked with an "R" and if not, it's the one on which the thread seems to rise to the right when you hold it up to the light.

3. Carefully align the right pedal's threaded stub with the threaded hole in the right crank (the one to which the chainrings are attached) and screw it in by hand as far as possible, turning clockwise ("to the right") as seen from the pedal side. If you notice resistance, make sure it's aligned properly—if necessary, start all over again.

4. Do the same with the left pedal on the left crank, turning it counterclockwise ("to the left").

5. Tighten both pedals fully using the wrench.

8

Using The Gears

MOST ADULT-SIZE BIKES sold these days are equipped with multi-speed gearing. Usually, that takes the form of a system with derailleurs that move the chain from one combination of front chainring and rear cog to another. Occasionally, you may see a bike with internal hub gearing, a single-speed bike without gears, and even more rarely you may encounter a bike with what's called a fixed wheel, meaning the cranks turn as long as the bike is moving, and there's no choice of gears either.

In this chapter, you'll learn how to use the gears on a bike with derailleur gearing. Except for the technical explanation of how derailleur gears work, what's covered here regarding gear selection also applies to bikes with hub gearing.

Fig. 8.1. Typical 24-speed derailleur system on a modern mountain bike. There are three chainrings on the right crank in the front and eight cogs on the freewheel in the back.

Both types of gearing have gone through a veritable revolution during the last 20 years. As recently as 1980, the norm for a bike with derailleur gearing was the "ten-speed," on which you had the choice between 2 chainrings at the cranks and 5 cogs at the rear wheel. And those things did not shift without some sophisticated skills on the rider's part. Today, most bikes sold are equipped with 18- or 24-speed gearing, with 2 ot 3 chainrings in front and 8 or 9 cogs on the rear wheel. What's even more significant, the modern derailleurs are much easier and more predictable in their shifting behavior than the old ones were.

The Parts of the Derailleur System

Mountain bikes, road bikes, hybrids, and touring bikes invariably use the derailleur gearing system. It is controlled by shifters, usually mounted on the handlebars, which operate the derailleurs via flexible control cables. The right shifter controls the shifts with the rear derailleur; the left one, the shifts with the front derailleur. Usually, the shifters are indexed, which means that there are definite click stops for each of the gears, making it much easier to shift than it was on bikes built before about 1986.

In the front, there are usually two or three different size chainrings. In the back, most of the newest high-end road bikes have 9 cogs and mountain bikes have 8, while older and simpler bikes may have anything from 5 to 7 cogs to choose from. The different sizes of chainrings and cogs are defined by the number of teeth around their circumference. Front chainrings have anything from 28 to 56 teeth, while cogs can have anything from 11 to 34 teeth, depending on their position in the sequence, and the type of bike. On mountain bikes, a typical setup will have chainrings with 24, 34, and 44 teeth, and cogs ranging from 11 through 28 teeth. A road bike typically has chainrings with 42 and 52 teeth and cogs ranging from 11 to 24 teeth, while hybrids and touring bikes typically use a configuration that is similar to the ones used on mountain bikes.

The highest gear will be the one on which the biggest chainring is combined with the smallest cog; the lowest gear combines the smallest chainring with the biggest cog. All other combinations fall somewhere in between.

Gearing Theory

The different gears are selected to compensate for variations in terrain. If you use the gears properly, you can maintain a fairly constant pedaling rate of perhaps 80 rpm (revolutions per minute) and a fairly constant pedaling force, while varying the bike's speed to match the difficulty of the terrain. Going downhill, select a high gear, which translates to a high riding speed for a given pedaling rate. Uphill, select a low gear, resulting in a lower riding speed at the same pedaling rate, keeping the force you have to apply to the pedals comfortable.

The easiest way to think of your gear is the distance you travel per crank revolution. A high gear lets you cover a greater distance for each crank revolution, making it faster and harder to push. A low gear lets you cover less terrain, making it slower and easier.

To be able to compare just how high or low a gear is, gear ratios are expressed by what is called a "gear number" in inches. This figure represents the theoretical wheel diameter of an equivalent directly driven wheel. The number can be read off

Fig. 8.2. Gearing combinations. Combining a big chainring with a small cog results in a high gear; a small chainring with a large cog gives a low gear.

Fig. 8.3. These are the crossover gear combinations. Don't use them, because they increase chainring and cog wear and cause poor shifting.

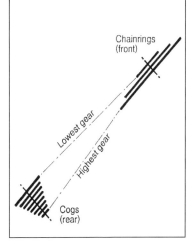

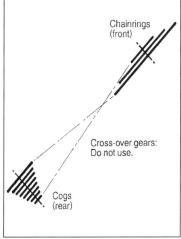

from a chart that's available at most bike shops, or it can be calculated as follows:

Gear number in inches =
(wheel diameter in inches) x (teeth on chainring)/(teeth on cog)

As an example, if your mountain bike with 26-inch wheels has a biggest chainring of 44 teeth and a smallest cog with 11 teeth, the resulting highest gear is 26 x 44/11 = 104 inches. If your smallest chainring has 24 teeth and the biggest cog also has 24 teeth, your lowest gear will be 26 x 24/24 = 26 inches.

Gearing Practice

Don't cross-chain; keep spinning; and change to the appropriate gear before it's too late. That is the short course in gearing. Now for what that means:

Don't cross-chain means that you should not use the gear combinations on which the chain runs from one extreme position in the front to the opposite extreme position in the rear. Take a look at your gearing setup. In the front, the smallest chainring is on the inside, the biggest on the outside. In the back, the smallest cog is on the outside, the biggest on the inside. So avoid running the chain across from the small (inside) chainring to the small (outside) cog, or from the big (outside) chainring in the front to the big (inside) cog in the back. In those gears, the chain would be twisted sideways too far and that causes excessive resistance, noise, and wear. This may also overextend the rear derailleur,

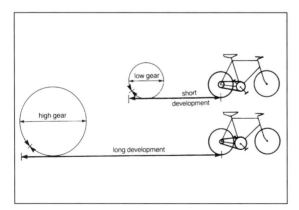

Fig. 8.4. In the low gear (top), one crank revolution takes you forward by a short distance. In the high gear (bottom), each crank revolution takes you a long way, requiring a greater effort but resulting in a higher riding speed.

causing it to fail and making the chain skip.

Put the bike up on a stand or support it any other way with the rear wheel off the ground, while the cranks are free to turn. Turn the cranks, and keep turning them. Shift with the right-hand shifter while looking at the rear derailleur. Note when the derailleur engages the biggest cog (low gear), and when it engages the smallest (high gear). Repeat until you remember what's what. Then do the same with the left-hand shifter, while watching the front derailleur. Practice until you know when the front derailleur puts the chain on the biggest chainring (high gear), and when on the smallest (low gear). Make a mental note of the shifter positions that correspond to the two cross-chain combinations, big-big and small-small, and remember not to use them when you're out riding the bike.

Now take the bike out on the road—better yet, on an empty parking lot. Ride it around and repeat all those shifting combinations. Note also that shifts are smoothest if you keep pedaling but reduce the force on the pedals while shifting.

Finally, take the bike into hilly terrain. Start off on level ground, selecting an intermediate gear (for example, an intermediate cog in the back with the middle chainring on a mountain bike, or the smaller of the two chainrings on a road bike). When you've gathered speed, shift up a notch with the right shifter (rear derailleur), and another notch. Then also shift with the left-hand shifter (front derailleur). When you go uphill, shift down; when you go downhill, shift up.

Now that you at least know what to do, start working on developing a feel for just when to do it. Try to maintain a relatively high pedaling rate (at least 60 rpm, preferably more, under most circumstances short of a very steep climb). When the bike starts going uphill, shift before you've lost momentum and start to slow down. Practice consciously until you feel you've mastered the trick, and you'll be a much more competent cyclist. You'll enjoy your riding and you won't tire as fast as riders who have not practiced shifting.

9

Getting Familiar with Your Bike

YOU'VE got your bike and your helmet, you know how the gears work, and now you're going to use that bike. To ride any new bike most effectively, I suggest you first practice some elementary handling skills, even if you've ridden bikes before, especially if your new bike is of a different type from your previous bike.

The reason why this is worthwhile, and in some cases essential, is that different types of bikes have quite different riding characteristics. That applies not only to the way they balance and steer, but also to the way they brake.

Even if you bought a mountain bike designed for the great outdoors, it'll be smarter to first practice under less demanding circumstances. An empty parking lot is ideal.

Repeat the entire practice program at least three times. Do it once on the first day. Go for an easy ride the next time you ride, paying attention to the situations where you can apply the lessons you've learned. The next time you take the bike out, devote the session to practice again. Then go on a slightly more challenging ride, followed by one more practice session, and you'll probably be ready for serious bike riding with a high level of competence and a thorough familiarity with your bike.

Check It Out

First do a dry run. Without getting on the bike, check over the entire bike. Do a check as described under "Pre-Ride Inspection" in Chapter 11, starting on page 82. Are the tires inflated properly and are the wheels held in firmly with the quick-releases? Is the seat at the right height and firmly in place; ditto for the handlebars? Are the brake cables attached at the brakes, and does pulling the lever lock the wheel? Can you shift into each of the gears while turning the cranks forward with the rear wheel lifted off the ground? Are any accessories firmly attached? If any of these things are found wanting, get them corrected before riding the bike.

Riding Practice

Before starting the next practice session, put your helmet on and adjust it properly, because you may fall. And if you do, be grateful you did this practice first, because it would surely

Fig. 9.1. Brake check. Load the bike with your weight and try to push it forward as you apply the brakes.

Fig. 9.2. This is the way to check whether the handlebars are on tight and straight.

mean you would have fallen under real-life riding conditions, which are much less controlled, on the road or the trail. Practice until you are fully comfortable and competent at handling the bike, and thus much less prone to falls and other accidents.

Get on the bike on a level stretch and ride a straight line. Try starting off in different gears and note how different it feels, and decide which gear you find most suitable for starting off (at least on level ground). Ride and shift into all the gears in sequence—up and down, and up again, until you've developed a feel for each gear under these circumstances. Try to keep your pedaling rate up to at least 60 rpm, and aim for 80 rpm.

Braking Practice

When practicing with the gears, you'll have used the brakes and you'll have made steering corrections, but now it's time to hone those skills separately and consciously.

When going straight at about walking speed, suddenly apply the rear brake. Note how the rear wheel probably skids? That's not good, because the brakes are only effective and predictable when the tires do not skid. So now get a feel for just how firmly you can apply that rear brake lever without skidding, but braking as firmly as possible. This gives you a reference for braking on level ground with a similar surface (you'll skid even sooner on a wet road or one with sand on it).

Now brake firmly, and just as you feel you're about to start skidding, back off on the lever a little. That's how you keep the brake and the bike under control.

Do the same with the front brake only. But be very alert to immediately release the front brake's lever when you notice the rear wheel starts to lift off the ground—a phenomenon known as "pitchover," also called "endo," and a potential cause of a serious fall if you don't control it by releasing the front brake lever immediately.

Next use both brakes simultaneously. Practice until you've developed a good feel for the way your bike's braking system, and the entire bike, responds to the force and suddenness of the brake lever application.

Steering Practice

To get a feel for the way your bike steers, just walk the bike holding it at the saddle, with one hand ready to steady the handlebars if needed. First try to follow a straight line and notice how you have to tilt the bike to the left or the right a little to correct its path each time it begins to deviate: if the bike starts veering to the left, you tilt it to the left; if it veers to the right, tilt it to the right to get it to straighten out. That's what also happens while you are riding, and it helps if you have an understanding of it.

Now get on the bike and try to ride a straight line, paying attention to the body lean and steering corrections you have to make. When you have developed a feel for it, continue by riding a wavy line—left, right, left, and so on.

Then move on to more distinct steering maneuvers. Ride a straight line and then, at a predetermined point, make a turn to the left or the right—again until you know how the bike responds while steering a gradual curve. Then do it at a higher speed, again noticing any difference in necessary steering and leaning corrections. (Notice that you lean over much more at low speeds than when going fast.)

To perfect your handling skills, you can learn the trickiest thing—making an abrupt turn. That's done by first briefly steering in the opposite direction (to make the bike lean over in the direction you want to go), and then immediately correcting by steering quite sharply into the direction you wanted to go in the first place. This is called the "forced" turn and it's very useful to avoid suddenly appearing obstacles, whether on the road or off-road.

For the next exercise it is doubly important to make sure you're prepared to let go of the brake levers, especially the one for the front brake. Apply the brakes when riding a curve instead of going straight. First do it, *gently*, just with the rear brake, and let go of the lever if you notice the wheel starts skidding—sideways this time. Notice how you regain control, not by braking more vigorously, but by actually letting go of the brake.

Do the same with the front brake, very gently. If you apply it too forcefully, the rear wheel starts to lift off and you'll lose control over the bike. If that should happen, respond by releasing the brake lever immediately. The message is, don't use the front brake in a curve, and if you do, be prepared to let go of it as soon as the bike even hints at erratic behavior.

Next, combine the use of the brake with the act of balancing—try to stand still while balancing on the bike. To do that, come to a gradual stop while trying to maintain your balance. Hold just the front brake, letting go of it just a touch if necessary, while you keep both feet on the pedals with the cranks in the horizontal position. If you begin to tip over one way, steer in that same direction and lean in the opposite direction, then release the brake a little to roll forward, helping you regain your balance. Standing still while on the bike may not seem a very useful skill, but what this really does is give you a good feel for balancing the bike.

Different Terrain

Once you are riding on a regular basis, it's a good idea to repeat each one of the preceding exercises on a sloping surface, both riding uphill and downhill. Make mental notes of the differences in bike behavior under these different circumstances.

Finally, if you intend to ride in rough terrain, practice on different surfaces as well—gravel roads, muddy tracks, slickrock, washboard surfaces, soft sand, even on snow and ice if you live in a region where it gets cold enough in winter.

10

Safe Cycling

W ATCH OUT FOR THE CARS. That was the extent of safety instruction I received from my parents when I got my first bike. Translated into today's world, that may have been, "Always wear your helmet." Makes good sense, but falls far short of an adequate preparation for safe cycling. I, for one, soon learned that running into a parked car while anxiously watching out for moving ones was a quick way of earning my first ride in an ambulance, and you may experience something similar if you put all your faith in that helmet and not enough in using its content—your head.

If you think you bought a mountain bike and you're going to ride it off-road, and therefore don't have to worry about any of this, think again. Cycling-related injuries of most types are about as likely to occur off-road as on the road. True, you're not likely to be hit by a car, but out in nature there are equally formidable risks, and most of the material covered in this chapter will apply off-road as much as it does if you ride mainly on paved roads.

The vast majority of bicycle injuries, including the most severe, are the result of the rider falling off the bike. Whether or not another party is involved—a motor vehicle, a bicycle, a pedestrian, or an animal—your skill in keeping control over the bike is crucially important.

Most accidents happen where there are others around—in other words, on the road—because that's where most cycling is done. Per mile ridden, separate bike paths are at least as accident-prone as regular roads. Even off-road, in terrain only accessible to mountain bikers, you'll be at risk.

The seriousness of the accident is of course another factor. The majority of very serious and fatal accidents involve head injury, many of those as the result of a collision with a motor vehicle. So, although that helmet won't ward off any accidents, it certainly tends to lessen the injury level of any fall on your head. Wear your helmet, and stay just as alert as you would be if you were not wearing it.

Let's divide all injuries into two groups—those resulting from falls and collisions with stationary objects, and those resulting from collisions with moving objects (motor vehicles, cyclists, pedestrians, and animals). The first category is referred to as "single participant accidents," the second one as "multiple participant accidents."

Single Participant Accidents

The way to prevent this category is to learn to handle your bike, and the basics of that were outlined in Chapter 9, "Getting Familiar with Your Bike." In addition to mastering the maneuvering skills associated with balancing, steering, and braking, you'll also have to work on your level of awareness. Think about what you're doing, where you're going, what may be in your path, and how you have to react to follow a safe path or avoid suddenly appearing obstacles. Consciously continue to practice and perfect your skills with the exercises described in Chapter 9 on pages 73 through 76. Eventually, you'll gain the level of experience that helps you avoid falls and accidents (and makes riding a bike more fun).

Be aware of the particular kind of hazard you're likely to encounter, and prepare for it. In wet weather off-road, you'll have to deal with muddy terrain, and you should expect not only to get stuck in muddy puddles, but also to be aware of the deterioration of brake performance in wet weather.

On slick surfaces, you're more likely to skid, causing loss of control when braking, steering, or accelerating. You can control that risk by not doing anything very abruptly—don't lean into the curves too much (take them gently rather than suddenly), brake gently, and accelerate gradually.

On rough and loose surfaces, you'll encounter similar problems as with slick surfaces, but they're even more unpredictable if you're not fully aware of the surfaces. Learn to judge where the terrain is loose and where there's a solid patch. Use this information to decide where you can safely turn, brake or accelerate, and where you have to avoid such maneuvers.

Particularly tricky are ridges in the surface that run diagonally across your path. Even worse are those that run parallel to it and so close that you have difficulty avoiding getting caught in them. Examples are erosion ruts on unpaved trails and railway tracks on roads.

The trick is to cross them perpendicularly with the bike upright. Achieve that by making the necessary diverting maneuver well ahead of the problem, and straightening out the bike *before* you get there, staying upright long enough by correcting your path only *after* you have safely crossed it. On the open road, make sure nobody's following you so closely as to be a threat to your, or the other party's, safety when you make the maneuver, and perhaps later have to veer out into the road farther than your regular path. Slow down and let the vehicle following pass first if necessary.

Multiple Participant Accidents

Most of the accidents in this category are highly avoidable. After all, they involve two parties and each party has a chance of taking avoiding action. The message is: use your head, and don't only think of what you're about to do, but also think about how it affects others, and how you can avoid an accident potentially caused by the other participant's mistake.

The first and simplest rule is to be predictable. Stay on a steady course, and don't do anything that forces you into a position from which you'll have to make a sudden diversion. An example is riding along a road with parked cars. Stay on a straight course far enough from those cars not to be endangered by doors suddenly opening. If you skip in and out between parked cars, following motorists will not be aware that you may suddenly have to move some six feet toward the center of the road, and you put yourself into jeopardy every time you do.

The second rule is to look. Look behind you before you start out and before making any maneuver that may interfere with the path of following drivers or cyclists. If someone is close enough to be hindered or endangered by your maneuver, wait until he or she has passed you. To alert those who are farther behind, give a hand signal to indicate what you're about to do. Legal hand signals for cyclists include extending the right arm for a right turn in most states of the U.S. (and probably just about everywhere else with right-hand traffic). Check your state's driver's handbook if you're in doubt. Where the extended right arm is not legal, you'll be expected to raise your left hand up to signal a right turn. To indicate that you're about to slow down or stop, swing the left arm up and down (the right hand in countries with left-hand traffic). To turn left, extend the left arm.

Even more important than those signals is your position in the road as a predictor of what you're about to do. If you want to go straight at an intersection, don't hug the outside edge of the road, but move boldly into the middle of the appropriate lane after having looked behind you and judged a safe time to do so. To turn left, depending on the number of separate traffic lanes, move close to the center of the road or into a lane dedicated to left-turning traffic. Again, if you're riding in a country with left-hand traffic, make the logical corrections to these instructions.

Finally on this subject, learn to interpret the other drivers' behavior for clues to their future actions. A car that's hugging the curb probably intends to turn right, and one close to the center of the road probably intends to turn left. Slowing down suggests uncertainty, and perhaps a sudden stop. Move into a position in which you are not going to run into that car if it does stop. Don't do anything abruptly, and always first look to make sure it's safe to carry out your maneuver.

People make mistakes. Others do, and if you're human, you will too at some point. In traffic, we're all dependent on an intricate interaction between different people, each of whom should be willing to make allowances for one another's mistakes. As a cyclist, you're more fragile and vulnerable than most other traffic participants. That probably means you have to give in to other people's mistakes, and even aggressive behavior, more often than you would in a car. Accept that as a fact of life, and take every action necessary to avoid endangering both yourself and others, even if the other driver is "at fault."

11

Routine Maintenance

BY ALL MEANS, take your bike back to the bike shop where you bought it for initial adjustments and major repairs. However, I also suggest you keep a little maintenance work "in house." It will help you understand your bike and its components, and that's half the battle of getting the most out of it.

In this chapter, you'll learn about a simple three-part maintenance program that you can carry out yourself and will ensure your bike is always in top shape. Even if you can't correct some of the problems you encounter, at least you'll know what needs to be done. This way, you'll be able to communicate clearly to a bike mechanic to get it taken care of.

The maintenance program described here consists of simple checks to be carried out at regularly scheduled intervals:

❑ Pre-ride inspection (each day you ride the bike)

❑ Monthly inspection

❑ Seasonal inspection (just once a year if you only ride the bike during the summer months)

In addition to these three inspections, you'll be shown how to clean the bike. That's something I recommend doing at least with each monthly inspection, but preferably whenever you've ridden the bike in wet weather or muddy terrain.

You can do the basic inspections without any tools. However, you will need to refer to the "Tools and Spares" section of Chapter 5, on page 53, for the tools you'll need to make any required corrections. In addition, you'll need cleaning cloths—one clean and dry, one damp, one greasy; brushes; thin penetrating oil in a spray can; special chain lubricant; bike polish; and a can of car wax.

Cleaning the Bike

Do this job whenever your bike gets dirty, preferably at least once a month, and before you take it to the shop for maintenance or repair service. It is much easier to work on a clean bike, and sometimes it's all it takes to solve a problem. Even this seemingly mundane job requires some thought, proceeding perhaps as follows.

Cleaning Procedure:

1. If the bike is dry, wipe it with a soft brush or a cloth to remove any dust and other dry dirt. If the bike or the dirt that adheres to it is wet, hose or sponge it down with plenty of clean water. Take care not to get water into the bearings of hubs, bottom bracket, pedals, and headset.

2. Using a damp cloth, clean in all the hard-to-reach nooks and crannies. Wrap the cloth around a screwdriver to get into hidden places, such as between the sprockets on the freewheel, between the chainrings, and around the derailleur pulleys.

3. Clean and dry the entire bike with a clean, soft, dry cloth.

4. Treat all the bare metal areas very sparingly with wax to inhibit rust, and rub it out with a clean, dry cloth.

5. Once or twice a year, it may be worthwhile to apply bike polish or wax to the paintwork as well.

6. To clean oxidation of bare metal, use chrome polish. For protection, the best thing to use is wax.

Pre-Ride Inspection

These are the things you ought to look out for whenever you take the bike out for a ride.

Tires:

Check whether the tires are inflated as marked on the tire sidewall, verified with a pressure gauge.

Handlebars:

Make sure the handlebars are straight, at the right height, and firmly attached. Check this by straddling the front wheel and trying to twist the handlebars.

Saddle:

Verify that the saddle is straight and level, at the right height, and firmly in place. It should not budge when you try twisting it relative to the frame.

Right: Fig. 11.1. Cleaning in tight corners, using a cloth wrapped around a screwdriver.

Below: Fig. 11.2. Adjusting the brake cable tension, shown here for a mountain bike. On a road bike, the adjusting barrel is on the brake itself.

Bottom right: Fig. 11.3. Make sure the brake pads completely touch the sides of the rim this way.

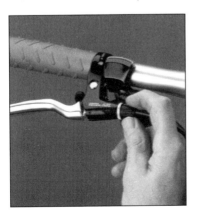

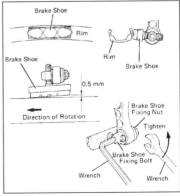

Brakes:

Check the effectiveness of the brakes by verifying that each can block the wheel against your weight with the lever depressed, leaving about 2 cm (¾ inch) between brake lever and handlebars, while you try to push the bike forward under your own weight.

Gears:

Lift the rear wheel and, while turning the cranks, check whether the derailleurs can be shifted to reach all the gears.

Monthly Inspection

Do this work at least once a month during the time you use the bike. First clean it as explained on page 82. Then carry out the Inspections listed above, and do the following additional jobs.

Wheels:

Check for broken spokes and wheel wobble. Lift the wheel off the ground and turn it slowly, keeping an eye on a fixed point such as the brake blocks. If the wheel seems to wobble sideways relative to the fixed point, it should be trued at a bike shop.

Brakes:

Adjust the cable tension as shown in Fig. 11.2 if the brakes don't firmly stop the bike with about 2 cm (¾ inch) clearance between the brake levers and the handlebars. Observe what happens when you pull the brake levers. The brake blocks must touch the sides of the rims over their entire surface. Adjust the brake pads as shown in Fig. 11.3 if they don't.

Tires:

Check the tires for external damage and embedded objects. Remove anything that doesn't belong there, and replace the tire if it is badly worn, or the tube if it loses air.

Cranks:

Using the crank extractor tool or the large Allen wrench, tighten the crank bolts, as shown in Fig. 11.4.

Overall Check:

Check all the other bolts and nuts on the bike to make sure they are tight. Verify whether all moving parts turn freely and all adjustments are correct. Repair or replace anything damaged or missing.

Lubrication

Lubricate the various parts listed here, using the lubricants indicated, and wipe any excess off afterwards.

Chain:	After the chain has been cleaned and dried, use a special non-gummy chain lube in a spray can.
Brake levers, pivots, cable ends:	Use a light spray can lubricant, aiming precisely with the little tubular nozzle installed on the spray head.
Exposed bare metal parts:	After cleaning with polish if it is tarnished, use car wax, applied with a soft, clean cloth and rubbed out to shine.

After lubrication, wipe off all excess lubricant, because exterior grease and oil deposits attract dirt and stain your clothes.

Seasonal Inspection

Although most bikes only need this work once or twice a year, you may have to do it more frequently if you ride a lot off-road in bad weather.

Procedure:

First carry out all the work described above for the monthly inspection on page 84, noting in particular which parts need special attention because they seem to be loose, worn, damaged or missing. Subsequently, work down the following list, getting anything that is necessary carried out at the bike shop (or learn to do it yourself with the help of a general bike maintenance book, such as my *Mountain Bike Maintenance* or *Road Bike Maintenance*).

Wheels:

With the wheels still in the bike, check for damage to the rims. Check the hubs for play, wear, and tightness. If there seems to be a problem, get it corrected.

Chain:

For a quick check, place the chain on the largest chainring in the front and try to lift an individual link off the chainring as shown in Fig. 11.5. Replace the entire chain if it can be lifted off by more than 3 mm ($^1/8$ inch). It means the chain is worn, which affects shifting and transmission efficiency. In addition, a worn chain also wears out the chainrings and cogs. If the chain is not badly worn, merely clean it with a general application of solvent applied with a brush. Wipe it off with a cloth and let it dry for no more than 15 minutes before lubricating it (it'll start rusting if you wait longer).

Bottom Bracket:

Check the bottom bracket bearings for play and freedom of rotation by grabbing the cranks and trying to twist and turn

Left: Fig. 11.4. Tightening the crank bolt with an 8 mm Allen wrench.

Below: Fig. 11.5. Replace the chain if it can be lifted off the chainring as shown here.

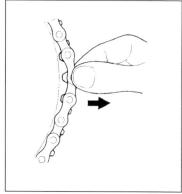

them. Get the unit overhauled or replaced if the spindle does not run perfectly smoothly or if there is noticeable play (looseness) in the bearings.

Pedals:

Check the pedals by holding them relative to the cranks and feeling them for play, then turn them to check for freedom of rotation. Replace or get them overhauled if they do not run smoothly or are too loose.

Headset:

Lift the front end of the bike by the frame's head tube and check to make sure the steering system turns freely, without either looseness ("play") or rough spots.

If it's a conventional headset, you need special headset tools. First loosen the top lockring, then tighten or loosen the upper headset race, and finally hold that in place while tightening the lockring again. Check once more and let a bike mechanic take care of it if the problem isn't solved.

If it's an Aheadset type, undo the handlebar stem binder bolts, tighten or loosen the Allen bolt on top of the stem, and tighten the stem's binder bolts again. Here too, get it fixed at a bike shop if you're not able to solve the problem yourself.

Derailleurs:

Clean, check, and lubricate both derailleur mechanisms, making sure the pivots work smoothly and the pulleys of the rear derailleur turn freely. If necessary, let a bike shop take care of any required corrections for you.

Shifters, Levers, and Cables:

Try out the brake levers and gear shifters, and make sure they operate smoothly. Check the cables to make sure there are no kinks in the cable mantles (also called cable housings) or frayed ends on the inner cables. If lubricating and adjusting does not make these mechanisms work smoothly and predictably, get them overhauled or replaced.

12

Basic Repairs

NO, THIS BOOK is not a repair manual, and you'll have to look elsewhere for extensive bicycle repair instructions (see the Bibliography on page 95). Just the same, there are a couple of problems that are so common that you ought to be able to fix them yourself, if only because that will help you get the bike back home before getting it fixed properly in a bike shop.

Don't tackle anything yourself that you don't feel comfortable with doing and aren't sure you understand how it works. If you're at all uncertain about what you've done, take the bike to the bike shop to have a professional fix it for you.

In this chapter, we'll cover the following simple repair jobs:

❑ puncture repair by replacing tube

❑ patch tube

❑ missing gear shifts

❑ loose crank

❑ poor braking

Fixing a Flat

Rather than show you how to patch a tube, we'll just cover the simpler method of replacing the inner tube. If you don't have a spare tube, or if you want to patch the puncture when you get home, see the following section, "Patching a Tube."

Tools and Equipment:

❏ set of tire levers

❏ pump, preferably also a tire pressure gauge

❏ spare tube

Procedure:

1. Remove the wheel from the bike, using the quick-release (or if the bike has bolt-on wheels, a fitting wrench), after releasing the brake cable at the brake or the lever. (Refer to pages 63–65 for wheel removal and reinstallation.)

2. If necessary, deflate the tube completely by pushing in the valve stem (in case of a Presta valve, first unscrew the little round nut at the tip of the valve).

Top left: Fig. 12.1. The first step in removing a tire: insert the tire lever under the tire bead and hook the other end on a spoke.

Bottom left: Fig. 12.2. Remove the tire by hand, or by pulling the tire lever around, to clear the bead over the edge of the rim.

Below: Fig. 12.3. Reinstall the tire by pulling it over the rim by hand. Ease the process by working the rest of the bead into the center of the rim.

3. Work one side of the tire into the deeper center of the rim, starting opposite the valve and working both ways toward it. The object is to loosen the tire bead in the area near the valve so it'll be easier to lift it off there.

4. Place a tire lever under the tire bead as shown in Fig. 12.1; use it to lift the tire bead up and hook the notch in the short end of the tire lever onto a spoke.

5. If the tire seems to lift off well, just grab the lever and pull it all the way around, pushing the rest of the bead off.

6. If it won't come off that easily, use the second tire lever about three spokes from the first one, then the third tire lever about three spokes in the other direction.

7. Now that side of the tire should be loose enough to lift it off the rim by hand over its entire circumference.

8. Push the valve through the hole in the rim from outside to inside. If it's held in place by a little round nut, remove that nut first.

9. Remove the rest of the tube from under the tire.

10. Check both the inside and the outside of the tire for any object that may have caused the puncture, and remove it. Also check to make sure the ends of the spokes are covered by the rim strip. If not, move the rim strip into position, or use several layers of adhesive tape to cover any projecting spoke ends.

11. Put the new tube in place under the tire, and insert the valve through the hole in the rim, then slightly inflate the tube. Reinstall the nut over the valve stem if one was installed.

12. Put the tire bead back over the rim by hand. If it seems too hard, let some air out of the tube and work the bead farther into the center of the rim. Start opposite the valve and work both ways toward the valve. The last section will be hard, but it can (and must) be done with your bare hands—don't use a tire lever, because that might damage the tube. If you don't succeed, ask someone at a bike shop to show you the trick.

13. Partially inflate the tire, knead it all around to put it the same distance between rim and the ridge on the sidewall, and inflate it to its final pressure.

14. Put the wheel back on the bike as explained on pages 64–65, making sure you center it properly, tighten the quick-release or axle nuts properly, and retension the brake.

Patching a Tube

This procedure is based on the tube being removed after following the instructions for the procedure on pages 89–91.

Tools and Equipment:

❑ tire patch kit

❑ pump

Procedure:

1. Try inflating the tube and check where air escapes. If it's not obvious, submerge it in water to see where air escapes. Dry the tube.

2. Sand, and then wipe, an area around the hole that's slightly bigger than the patch you'll be using.

3. Spread tire adhesive from the patch kit thinly and evenly over the area you just cleaned. Wait 2 minutes in warm weather, 4 minutes in cool weather.

4. Remove the aluminum foil backing from the adhesive side of the patch but leave the transparent plastic on the other side in place.

5. Place the patch on the tire, centered around the hole. Press it down firmly over its entire area. Stretch tube and patch together in several directions and make sure no part of the patch lifts off.

6. Inflate the tube to a moderate pressure and wait to make sure it holds air before reinstalling it.

Fix Gear Shift Problems

If the gears do not engage properly when shifting, first make sure it's not because you are trying to shift into one of the combinations you should avoid anyway because they cross the chain. If it happens with other gear combinations, find the adjusting barrel for the derailleur in question (front or rear).

1. With the shifters, select the gear that engages the largest chainring in the front with the smallest cog in the rear. Lift the rear wheel and turn the cranks forward. If it either does not work at all or only very noisily, find out what's not working properly—the front derailleur or the rear derailleur.

2. Adjust the cable adjuster for the derailleur that's not working. First turn it in half a turn and see whether it gets better. If it does, turn it in further or less far until it works properly. If it gets worse, turn the adjuster in the other direction and repeat until it's working correctly.

3. With the wheel off the ground, make all the shifts with the other derailleur, keeping the one you just adjusted in place. If necessary, also tighten or loosen the adjuster for this derailleur.

4. If whatever you do, the derailleur either "dumps" the chain, shifting beyond the smallest or biggest chainring or cog, or does not quite reach the biggest or smallest chainring or cog, adjust the derailleur's set-stop screws in accordance with steps 5 or 6 below.

Fig. 12.4. Detail of derailleur adjustment. To adjust the tension of the cable, screw the barrel adjuster in or out. The two little screws are adjusted to limit the range of travel of the derailleur.

5. Loosen or tighten the screw marked L to move the chain further or less far in the direction of the biggest cog (rear derailleur) or small chainring (front derailleur).

6. Loosen or tighten the screw marked H to move the chain further or less far in the direction of the smallest cog (rear derailleur) or big chainring (front derailleur).

Tighten Loose Crank

Sometimes, the cranks come loose as you are riding, especially on a new bike.

Tools and Equipment:

❑ wrench part of crank tool or 8 mm Allen wrench (depending on the type of crank bolt)

Procedure:

1. To avoid the problem, check the crank bolts at least once a week during the first month.

2. To do that, or to fasten it if it came loose anyway, first remove the dustcap, if installed.

Fig. 12.5. Detail drawing of crank attachment. To tighten the crank when it is loose, screw in the crank bolt.

Fig. 12.6. Adjusting the brake pad. The brakes only work properly if the brake pads touch the rims as shown in Fig. 11.3 on page 83.

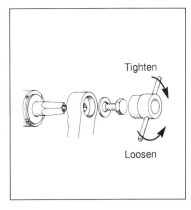

3. Tighten the crank bolt with the crank bolt tool (either an Allen wrench, if there was no dustcap; or the wrench part of the crank tool, if there was a dustcap).

4. Reinstall the dustcap, if one was installed.

Adjust Brake

If the brake does not seem to work adequately, first make sure the rims are not wet, dirty, or greasy.

Tools and Equipment:

❑ cloth or abrasive pad

❑ solvent

Procedure:

1. Thoroughly clean the sides of the rims where the brake pads rub, using a solvent and an abrasive pad if they were greasy.

2. If the brakes still don't work properly, try adjusting the cable tension.

3. To get more powerful braking, turn the cable adjuster out, effectively lengthening the cable casing a little, thus applying the brakes earlier.

4. Check to make sure the brake now does not rub against the side of the rim when it's not supposed to be engaged. If that's the case, turn the adjuster in a little until the optimum position is found.

5. When it's adjusted right, hold the barrel adjuster with one hand and tighten the locknut with the other.

6. If you can't solve the problem this way, take the bike to a bike shop or consult a repair manual.

7. If the brakes rub on the rims intermittently, get the wheel trued by a bike shop as soon as possible.

Bibliography

Berto, Frank J. *Bicycling Magazine's Complete Guide to Upgrading Your Bike.* Emmaus, PA: Rodale Press, 1988.

Coles, Clarence W., Harold T. Glenn, and John S. Allen. *Glenn's New Complete Bicycle Manual: Selection, Maintenance, Repair.* New York: Crown Publishers, 1989.

Cuthberson, Tom. *Anybody's Bike Book.* Berkeley, CA: Ten-Speed Press, 1998.

Edwards, Sally. *The Heart Rate Monitor Book.* New York: Polar, 1994.

Harrell, Julie. *A Woman's Guide to Buying a Bike.* San Francisco: Van der Plas Publications, 1999.

Henderson, J. *The Haynes Bicycle Book.* Osceola, WI: MBI Publishing, 1997.

Maffetone, Phil, and Matthew Mantell. *The High Performance Heart.* San Francisco: Bicycle Books, 1994.

Perry, David. *Bike Cult.* New York: Four Walls, Eight Windows, 1996.

Rafoth, Richard. *High Performance Bicycle Nutrition.* Osceola, WI: MBI Publishing, 1998.

Ries, Richard. *Building Your Perfect Bike.* Osceola, WI: MBI Publishing, 1996.

Rodriguez, Angel, and Carla Black. *The Tandem Book.* San Clemente, CA: Info Net Publishing, 1997.

Van der Plas, Rob. *The Bicycle Repair Book.* San Francisco: Bicycle Books, 1993.

———. *Bicycle Technology: Understanding, Selecting, and Maintaining the Modern Bicycle and its Components.* San Francisco: Bicycle Books, 1991.

———. *The Bicycle Touring Manual: Using the Bicycle for Touring and Camping.* Osceola, WI: MBI Publishing, 1993.

———. *Mountain Bike Maintenance: Repairing and Maintaining the Off-Road Bicycle.* San Francisco: Bicycle Books, 1994.———. *Road Bike Maintenance: Repairing and Maintaining the Modern Lighweight Bicycle.* San Francisco: Bicycle Books, 1996.

———. *Roadside Bicycle Repair: The Simple Guide to Fixing Your Bike.* San Francisco: Bicycle Books, 1995.

——— and Charles Kelly. *The Original Mountain Bike Book.* Osceola, WI: MBI Publishing, 1998.

Index

accessories, 48–53
  installation, 53
accidents, 77–81
acknowledgments, 5

bags, 51
bar-ends, 49
Bicycle Trader (magazine), 55
bike shops, 10, 54–57
BMX bike, 25
brake lever, 32–33
brakes, 32-33
  adjustment, 63, 93–94
braking practice, 74
brands, *see* manufacturers

Campagnolo, 35–37
chain, 33–34, 67–71, 86
chainrings, 34, 67–71
children, carrying, 52
cleaning, 82
clipless pedals, 33
clothing, 47–48
cockpit size, *see* front length
CO₂-inflator, 50
components, 29–37
cost, 14, 16–28,
  of used bikes, 57
  v. weight, 30–31
crank, 33–34
  length, 44
  tighten, 86, 92
cross-chain, 70–71
cross-country (mountain)
  bike, 17–18
cruiser, 23, 25
cyclo computer, 35, 51
cyclo-cross bike, 25

derailleurs, 34, 67–71
dirt bike, 25
downhill (mountain) bike,
  17–19
drivetrain, 33–34
drop-handlebars
  (road bike), 20

equipment
  for bike, 48–53
  for rider 45–48

fenders, 35
fixed-wheel bike, 26
flat (tire) repair, 88–92
folding bike, 26
fork, 32
frame, 31
  size, 39–40
freewheel, 34
front length, 42–43
front reflector bracket, 52

gear, (*also see* gearing)
  number, 69–70
  shifter adjusting, 63
  shift problems, 91–92
gearing, 17–18, 20, 34, 67–71
  parts of, 68
  practice, 70–71
  theory 69–70
gruppo, 27–29, 35–37

hand cycle, 28
handlebars, 32
  adjustment, 61–62
  height, 41–42, 61–63
  width, 42–44
  handling, 72–76
hand signals, 80
headset, 32, 41–42, 87
helmet, 7, 45–46, 77
HRM (heart rate monitor], 51
hybrid, 21–22

injuries, 77–81
inspection, 56–57, 73, 82–87

lights, 35, 50
lock, 49
luggage
  carrying of, 24, 51–52
  racks, 35, 51–52
lubrication, 85

magazines, 9
mail-order, 10
maintenance, 81–87
manufacturers
  of bikes, 9, 12–13
  of components, 35–37
  materials, 13
models (of bikes), 9, 12
mudguards, *see* fenders

parts of bike, 29–37
pedaling rate, 70–71
pedals, 33
  remove and install, 65–66
  personal preferences, 14
Phelan, Jacquie, 11
pump, 49–50
puncture (see flat)

quality, 13-14, 36–37
quick-release
  for seat, 60
  for wheel, 63–65

racks, 35, 51–52
raingear, 48
recreational (mountain)
  bike, 17–19
reflectors, 35, 52

mounting bracket, 52
repairs, 88–94
rim, 32
risks, 7, 77–80
road bike, 19–21
roadster, 24
recumbent, 28

Sachs, 36
saddle, 34–35, 43–44, 58–60
  adjustments, 59–60
  height, 41
  width, 43–44
safety, 7, 52, 77–80
seat, see saddle
seatpost, 41, 59–60
service, 10–11, 81–85, 88–94
Shimano, 29, 35–37
shops, 10–11, 55
shoes, 47
size (of bike), 13, 38–44
sizing equipment, 38
spinning, 70–71
SRAM, 36
steering system, 32
steering practice, 75–76
stem, 32, 41–42
standover height, *see*
  straddle height
straddle height, 39–40, 59–60
sunglasses, 48
sunscreen, 48
suspension, 16–19, 35

tandem, 27–28
terrain, effect on handling,
  76, 78–79
Terry Precision Cycling for
  Women, 43
theft, 55–56
three-speed bike, 24
time-trialing bike, 19–20
tire size, 18–21
tools, 53
touring bike, 22
track bike, 26
trailer, 52
trekking bike, 21
triathlon bike, 19–20
trials bike, 25
types of bike, 11–12, 15–28

used bikes, 23, 54–57
  sources, 55
utility bike, 23–24

water bottle, 49
weight, 14
wheel, 32
  remove, install, 63–65
women (special needs), 43